CU00820104

Epic English Words
Dictionary of Beauty, Interest, and Wonder

Robin Devoe

Epic English Words
Dictionary of Beauty, Interest, and Wonder

From Lazy R Softcovers, Spenard, Alaska
Edition Beta Prime – March 2022
ISBN #9798787547795
George G. Nagel, editor

Book Notes
Select pronunciations, plurals, and masculine or feminine forms are noted in (parentheses). [Bracketed] information appending entries may include etymology, country of origin, related words, etc. Foreign words in the [bracketed] etymology information are *italicized*, with meanings following. These words may be *etyma* or just cognates as in: [Latin *procella* storm] and [Italian *lacrima* tear], respectively. If an entry word itself is foreign (e.g., Zeitgeist), then often meaning is italicized instead, as in: [German *time spirit*]. Some entries include quotes showing word usage; some such quotes are from Robin Devoe's *Pale Western Star*. Unattributed quotes are original example sentences. Some entries from the more comprehensive *Dictionary of the Strange, Curious, and Lovely* are also included.

Abbreviations
adj. a*djective*; **AKA** *also known as*;
(B)CE *(Before) Common Era*; **c.** *century*;
e.g. *exempli gratia (for example)*; **esp.** *especially*;
incl. *including*; **m** meters; **myth.** *mythology*;
pl. *plural*; and **pop.** *population*.

Introduction: What is this Book?

This book is part dictionary, part very portable, extremely selective, and curated *encyclopedia*. Unusual and interesting vocabulary, but also terms from the sciences & arts; place names & literary references; linguistic curiosities; and names from mythology & zoology. This book showcases words and terms that are all interesting for some reason. Some look or sound beautiful; some are strange in a creative way; some esoteric and deep. Many entries include etymologies and quotations from poetry, literature, etc. showing word usage.

In populating this book, subjective taste was unavoidable. Why is a star such as Omicron Draconis chosen over other stars? Simply because the author fancies the name itself. Other entries are chosen due to unique features, or beauty of sound, appearance, or meaning. Included within are interesting places, real and mythological (Shitlington Crags, Shambhala, Muspelheim); names from zoology (dreamfish & wonderpus); cryptozoology (Mongolian death worm); astronomy (El Gordo & Aldebaran); music (protopunk & doodlesack); literature (Prufrockian & purple passages); history (Pavlopetri); mathematics (Whitney umbrella); terms from geology (inselberg & Devonian); and intriguing words such as welkin, smokefall, orison, omnishambles, nemorous, circumvolant, moonglade, meeping, goetic, esperance, cosmoplastic, brontide, and anagalactic. Some of the best entries from the more comprehensive *Dictionary of the Strange, Curious, and Lovely* are also included.

In addition to the many *recherché* vocabulary words, there are numerous entries from mythology, astronomy, geography, zoology, poetry, and literature. Just a few humans are listed as entries (e.g., Finnish poet *Runeberg* and English astrologer *Sepharial*). A liberal sprinkling of English's more elegant prefixes (such as: *circum-*, *cosmo-*, *proto-*, *ob-*, and *para-*) and suffixes (*-esque*, *-mancy*, *-escent*, *-ium*, and *-genic*) are spread throughout this alphabetized volume.

"Brevity is the soul of wit" – Shakespeare, *Hamlet*
This book was designed to be very portable, very casual –
yet intriguing & inspiring. The reader is gently introduced to
new & interesting words, to strange, beautiful, or elegant
words. If you love these types of words and terms, you will
likely love this collection! If you are looking, however, for
OED-type definitions with every word sense and
comprehensive etymology and pronunciations, this book
may not be for you.

The 9-page "Supplemental Words of Beauty or Interest"
appending this volume lists just the words themselves,
without definitions – most (but far from all) definitions are
relatively apparent or commonly known.

– Robin Devoe
Vale de Lune, Alaska – November, 2021

A

abnormous irregular; deformed; [Latin *abnormis*]

Abyssinia an old name for the Ethiopian Empire

abyssopelagic of or pertaining to the deep ocean or the abyssal zone; [Latin *pelagus* (the sea)]

acclivity (uh-KLI-vuh-tee) an upward slope; [adj. *acclivitous* or *acclivous*]; [Latin *clivus* slope]

acheronian or **acherontic** dismal and dark; [from *Acheron* in Greek myth., the river of sorrow in Hades that Charon ferried souls of the dead across]; "The intervening years are sucked down these *acheronian* halls like light into a black hole while you helplessly teeter upon the event horizon..." – Rick Yancey, American sci-fi author

acushla term of address; darling; [Irish *a chuisle* (O pulse)]

adharma immorality; unrighteousness; [Sanskrit]

Adonis blue a European butterfly

adorkable adorable in a socially awkward way; [blend of *adorable* and *dork*]; [informal]

adumbral dark; shady; [verb: *adumbrate*]

advesperate darken; become late; [Latin *vesper* evening]

aegipan a goat-like creature similar to a satyr – sometimes with a fish's tail; [classical myth.]

aeolian (ee-OH-lee-uhn) referring or relating to the wind; "The actor should not play a part. Like the *Aeolian* harps that used to be hung in the trees to be played only by the breeze, the actor should be an instrument played upon by the character he depicts." – Alla Nazimova, 20th c. Russian-American actress & director

Aeolian Islands a volcanic group with eight main islands in the Tyrrhenian Sea north of Sicily; [*Aeolus*, Greek god of the winds]

aeromancy divination by the state of the air; weather forecasting; [adj. *aeromantic*]

aestival or **estival** of, relating to, or appearing in the summer season

aestivate or **estivate** to spend the summer, as in a particular manner or at a particular place; to enter stasis during summer months; [noun: *aestivation*]; "For millennia, rulers of those warm lands had chosen to *aestivate* in the highlands."

Aether one of the first gods born from Chaos; the personification of the pure upper air that gods breathe, not the normal air mortals breathe; [Greek myth.]

aeviternal everlasting; endless

afflatus sudden rush of poetic or divine inspiration; [Latin *frattis* (to breathe)]; "Through me the *afflatus* surging and surging, through me the current and index." – Walt Whitman, 19th c. American poet

afforest to cover with forest; to turn into hunting grounds

Afriski a ski resort in Lesotho (southern Africa)

afterclap an unexpected, damaging, or unsettling after-effect or repercussion

agathodemon a benevolent spirit; [Ancient Greek *agathós* good]

Aidenn paradise; [from Hebrew *éden* and Arabic *adn*]; [poetic]

Aisling (ASH-ling) an Irish female given name meaning a vision or dream

alamort totally exhausted; half-dead from fatigue; [French *à la mort* (to the death)]; [obsolete]

Albion an old name for England, Britain, or the British Isles; [poetic]; [Latin *albus* white]; [likely named for the white cliffs of Dover]

alcazar any Moorish fortress in Spain; [Arabic *al-qasr* (the castle)]

Aldebaran a bright star in the constellation Taurus; [Arabic *ad-dabarān* (the follower)]; "The sovereign brilliancy of Sirius pierced the eye with a steely glitter, the star called Capella was yellow, *Aldebaran* and Betelgeux shone with a fiery red." – Thomas Hardy, *Far from the Madding Crowd*

Alexander's Band an area of darker sky between primary and secondary rainbows; [*Alexander* Aphrodisias, 3rd c. Greek philosopher]

alexandrine a twelve syllable line of iambic verse; "A needless *Alexandrine* ends the song / That, like a wounded snake, drags its slow length along." – Alexander Pope, 18th c. English poet

Alfheim a celestial domain inhabited by fairies and light elves; [Norse myth.]

Algerine alternative form of Algerian

Alph River a small river in an ice-free region of Antarctica; [also nearby: *Xanadu Hills*]; "In *Xanadu* did Kubla Khan
A stately pleasure-dome decree:
Where *Alph,* the sacred river, ran
Through caverns measureless to man
Down to a sunless sea." – Coleridge, *Kubla Khan*

Alphard the brightest star in the constellation Hydra – no other bright stars are nearby in the night sky; [Arabic *al-fard* (the individual)]

Altai-Sayan region a central Asian region near where Russia, Mongolia, China, and Kazakhstan meet – home to unique cultural, religious, and biological diversity; [*Altai* Mountains and *Sayan* Mountains]

altitonant thundering from on high; a person or thing thundering loudly from above; [adj. & noun]

altivolant flying high; [obsolete]

altocumulus castellanus a type of cloud named for its towering projections; may suggest an impending thunderstorm; [Latin *altus* (high) + *cumulus* (heaped) + *castellanus* (castle)]

amadelphous living in flocks; gregarious

amaranthine undying; immortal;
"Where *amaranthine* gardens gleam."
– Clark Ashton Smith, *Dominium in Excelsis*

amaryllis belladonna pink & white species of flower native to South Africa

American cave lion a pantherine cat ranging from Alaska to Mexico – extinct since 11,000 years ago

amphisbaena a mythical serpent with a head at both ends and able to move in both directions

amplexus the mating clasp of some male amphibians; [Latin *amplexus* embrace]

amrita the ambrosial syrup the drinking of which bestows immortality; drink of the Hindu gods; the water of life; [Hindu myth.]

anagalactic beyond our galaxy, as *anagalactic* worlds; [Ancient Greek *aná* (above, on, up)]

anagogic mystical; interpreting a thing as having a deeper, spiritual meaning; [Latin *anagoge* elevation]

Andean cock-of-the-rock the national bird of Peru

Andvaranaut a magic ring that can aid the search for gold; [Norse myth.]

anhedonic unable to experience pleasure; [noun: *anhedonia*]

anima (masculine: *animus*) in Jungian psychology, the true inner self of a person; the unconscious feminine aspect in men; [Latin *anima* soul]

Anima Mundi the vital force, or spiritual essence, of the world; [Latin *soul of the world*]

anomalistics the use of scientific methods to try and find a rational explanation for seemingly anomalous phenomena

anschluss any political union, but originally the one between Germany and Austria in 1938

antelucan before dawn or daylight; esp. applied to the predawn assemblage of early, persecuted Christians

antinatalism negative philosophical view towards having children; [noun: *antinatalist*]

apeirophobia fear of infinity; [Ancient Greek *ápeiros* infinite]

aperçu (ah-pear-sue) a clever insight; an initial view or rapid survey; a summary or outline; [French]

Apollonian related to the Greek god Apollo; clear, harmonious, ordered; restrained; serene and high-minded; opposite of *Dionysian*

appointment in Samarra one's death; [from W. Somerset Maugham's 1933 retelling of a Babylonian myth.]

apricate to bask in the sun; [Latin *apricus* sunny]

apricity sunshine; the sun's warmth in winter

aquiclude in geology, an impermeable layer above or below an aquifer; [Latin *aqua* (water) + *claudere* (to shut)]

Arabian mate a common checkmate pattern employing rook and knight to corner the mated king; [mentioned in ancient Arabic manuscripts]

Arcadian or **arcadian** ideally rustic or pastoral; peaceful and simple; a utopian realm of great natural beauty and boundless pleasures both spiritual and physical; [from the ancient Greek region *Arcadia*]

Archimedean point or **God's-eye view** a hypothetical viewpoint from which objective truth can be clearly perceived; a perfectly objective point of view; [from the supposed claim of ancient Greek mathematician *Archimedes* that he could move the Earth if given a place to stand, a solid point, and a lever long enough]

Archimedes's mirror array of mirrors Archimedes supposedly used to create a heat ray and burn the sails of Roman ships attacking the Hellenistic city of Syracuse (on Sicily) in 213 BCE

archly in a knowing, clever, or mischievous manner; slyly

archmage (pl. *archmagi*) a very powerful wizard or sorcerer

archosaurian belonging to or like a subclass of mostly extinct reptiles which includes dinosaurs, pterosaurs, and crocodilians

Arcturus brightest star in the northern celestial hemisphere; [Ancient Greek *arktos* (bear) + *ouros* (guardian)]

argent silver-colored; [Latin *argentum* silver]

argentiferous silver-bearing; [French *argent* silver]

Argentine, the the country of Argentina

argillaceous containing clay; clay-like; [Latin *argilla* clay]

Argo the mythic ship Jason & the Argonauts sailed in quest of the golden fleece;

> "A loftier *Argo* cleaves the main,
>   Fraught with a later prize;
> Another Orpheus sings again,
>   And loves, and weeps, and dies.
> A new Ulysses leaves once more
> Calypso for his native shore." – Shelley, *Hellas*

Argo Chasma an estimated 6-mile deep canyon on Charon, a satellite of dwarf planet Pluto

argonaut one on a dangerous but perhaps highly rewarding quest

argot (ar-go) a secret language or slang peculiar to thieves, vagabonds, or any particular group; [adj. *argotic*]

aristology the art or science of fine eating; [Ancient Greek *áriston* (breakfast, lunch)]

armisonant resounding with noises of arms or battle

Arrakis Planitia a large plain on Saturn's moon Titan – Titanean plains are named after planets from Frank Herbert's work; [official name of the desert planet in the novel *Dune* + Latin *plānitia* (plain)]

aspenglow alpenglow; reddish glow (often post-sunset) on mountain summits

aspheric almost a perfect sphere

asphodel a Mediterranean flowering plant; in Greek myth., the flower carpets Hades, which the dead feed upon; [Ancient Greek *asphódelos*];

> "With her ankles sunken in *asphodel*
> She wept for the roses of earth which fell."
> – Elizabeth Barrett Browning, 19th c. English poet

Asphodel Meadows that part of the Underworld where ordinary people live and are treated neutrally, in contradistinction to the everlasting joy experienced by heroes in *Elysium*; [Greek myth.]

asterism a small group of stars that form a visible pattern but are not an official constellation, e.g. the Summer Triangle or Orion's Belt

astraphobia an abnormal fear of thunder and lightning

astrobleme a scar or crater on the Earth's surface caused by a meteorite impact

astrogate to navigate in outer space, as a spaceship between stars or planets; [adj. *astrogational*]

asyla alternative plural form of asylum (also asylums)

ataraxia perfect peace of mind; perfect calmness; [adj. *ataraxic*]

atrabilious or **atrabilarious** inclined to melancholy; [Latin *ātra bīlis* (black bile)];
"The music of her lute is an endless flood
of smooth-flowing baptism,
transporting us beyond this *atrabilious* plane."
– Robin Devoe, *Alexandra Rustaveli*

atramental like ink; relating to ink; black

Augean extremely filthy; [Hercules had to divert the river Alpheus to cleanse the stables of *Augeas*]; [Greek myth.]

aulic pertaining to a royal court

aurocephalous having a gold-colored head, such as many birds; [Latin *aurum* gold + *cephalicus* head]

aurora polaris either northern lights (*aurora borealis*) or southern lights (*aurora australis*); usually seen in high-latitude areas

austral related to or coming from the south; southern

Avalon legendary island paradise somewhere in the western seas (esp. in the British Isles) noted for beautiful apples; also where King Arthur is buried (or lies asleep, to awaken at some future time)

Avalonia a microcontinent in the Paleozoic era – its crustal fragments underlie parts of Great Britain, Ireland, and North America

avatar material embodiment of an idea; a personification; a digital representation of a person or being; in Hinduism, the earthly manifestation of a deity, esp. Vishnu; [Sanskrit *avatāra* (descent of a deity from a heaven)]; "Thinking of love beneath the stars
She feels a Heaven touch the earth:
Like twenty thousand golden *avatars*
streaming down to a mortal birth."
– Robin Devoe, *Avatars of Gold*
Aventine Hill southernmost of ancient Rome's seven hills
aviatrix (pl. *aviatrices*) a female aviator
azan or **adhan** the call to prayers in Islam
Azrael the Angel of Death in Islam and in some Jewish belief systems
azuline or **azurn** a shade of blue
azure the clear blue color of the sky; the blue vault above; the unclouded sky;
"He clasps the crag with crooked hands;
Close to the sun in lonely lands,
Ring'd with the *azure* world, he stands."
– Alfred, Lord Tennyson, *The Eagle*
azured of an azure color; sky-blue;
"The *azured* harebell." – Shakespeare, *Cymbeline*

B

Baade's Window an area of space with less interstellar dust, allowing better observation of the Galactic Center of the Milky Way; [German astronomer Walter *Baade*]
Babylonic related to or from Babylon – capital of the ancient kingdom of Babylonia; tumultuous; [derived from Akkadian *Bābilim* (Gate of God)]
Bacchic jovial; related to riotous intoxication; drunken; [from *Bacchus*, the Roman god of wine]
Baldr a good god, loved by all – Loki tricked Balder's blind brother Hoder into killing him; [Norse myth.]
balter to dance or walk clumsily or without grace

Baltis Vallis a winding channel on Venus – longest known channel in the Solar System; [Syrian *Baltis* (planet Venus) + Latin *vallis* (valley)]

bandersnatch a fast, ferocious, long-necked, and fictional creature; [from Lewis Carroll]

barathrum a deep pit in Athens, into which condemned criminals were tossed; an abyss; hell; one who is insatiable

Barmecidal (bar-muh-SIDE-il) providing only the illusion of plenty or abundance; [from a story in *One Thousand and One Nights*, where a prince offers a beggar a feast that is only imaginary]

Bastardo a central Italian village; [shortened from *Osteria del Bastardo* (Bastard's Inn) in the 1920's]

bathos (BAY-thos) a ridiculous descent from the sublime to the commonplace in writing or speech; an anticlimax, perhaps with humorous effect; sentimentality; [adj. *bathetic*]; [Greek *báthos* depth]; "This curious blend of the sublime and the *bathetic* does not come again until Kafka..." – Harold Bloom, American literary critic

Battle of the Eclipse 585 BCE battle between the Medes and Lydians in what is now Turkey – an eclipse during the battle led to an immediate peace deal

beard-second the length a beard grows in one second – about 10 billionths of a meter

bearded dragon common name for *Pogona* – a genus of reptiles that includes six Australian lizard species that grow up to two feet long

beau sabreur a dashing swordsman or gallant adventurer; [French *handsome swordsman*]

beavered wearing a beaver hat; bearded

beblubber to make swollen and disfigured by weeping; [adj. *beblubbered*]

beestings the first milk from a cow (or other mammal) after it has given birth

before times the period of time before a major, defining event, esp. a catastrophic world-changing event such as a large meteorite impact

Bellatrix the third brightest star in the constellation Orion; [Latin *warrior woman*]

Belle Époque, La the period in French history from roughly 1875-1914 (the start of WWI); characterised by optimism, economic prosperity, and scientific, technological & cultural innovation; [French *the Beautiful Epoch*]

Bellerophon or **Bellerophontes** ancient Greek hero that slayed the *Chimera* and earned the gods disfavor by trying to fly Pegasus to Mount Olympus; [Greek myth.]

belliferous bringing war; [Latin *bellum* war]

belligerati well-educated people, esp. authors, who promote unnecessary wars of aggression; [*belligerent* + *literati*]

belling sound of a male deer during mating season

bellipotent mighty in war

belt of Venus or **Venus's girdle** or **antitwilight arch** an atmospheric phenomenon visible shortly after sunset (or before sunrise), consisting of a vivid pinkish glow extending 10-20 degrees above the horizon (in winter), or a yellow-orangish band nearer the horizon (in summer)

bene darkmans an evening or nighttime farewell; similar to "good night"; [British]; [obsolete]

Benelux Union the politico-economic union between the Low Countries; [**Be**gium, **Ne**therlands, and **Lux**umbourg]

bergfall an avalanche largely composed of rock; the fall of mountain rocks; [German *Berg* mountain]

bergschrund crevasse at the head of many alpine glaciers; [German *mountain cleft*]

bergwind a hot, dry wind blowing toward the coast; [Afrikaans]

bibcock a faucet or tap with nozzle bent downwards

Bifrost the burning, rainbow bridge connecting Asgard (heaven) with Midgard (earth); [Norse myth.]

biogenic created or produced by live organisms or by biologic processes; necessary to perpetuate life processes (e.g., food & water) for mammals

biomorphic resembling or suggesting the curving, irregular forms of living organisms, rather than an artistic ideal

biospheric of or relating to the regions of Earth containing life or to all living organisms and their environment

Black Dragon Fire, The a 1987 fire (the largest to strike China in 300 years) that killed hundreds, unhoused thousands, spread into Russia, and destroyed 1/6 of China's timber reserves

blake pale; wan; [Northern England; poetic]

blue hour twilight when the sun's below the horizon and indirect sunlight takes on a blue shade

blue men of the Minch or **storm kelpies** mythological creatures living in waters near the Outer Hebrides; malevolent, they create storms and lie asleep just beneath the sea's surface during fine weather; [The *Minch*, a Scottish strait]

Blue Snowball Nebula a planetary (observed as round) nebula in the constellation Andromeda

bodhi in Buddhism, the state of highest enlightenment; [Sanskrit]

bogglish doubtful; skittish

bogle goblin; spectre; phantom; a fearsome thing

bombinate to make a humming or buzzing sound; [derived from Ancient Greek *bómbos* (booming, humming)]

booboisie (boob-wa-ZEE) boobs as a class; a large portion of the general public regarded as consisting of uncultured or ignorant boobs; [play upon *bourgeoisie*]; [slang]

boomslang poisonous African tree snake; [Afrikaans *boom* (tree) + *slang* (snake)]

boondock a remote, rural area – usually brushy; [Tagalog *bundok* mountain]

boreal of or relating to the North, the forested areas of the North, or the north wind; northern; [*Boreas*, the Greek

god of the north wind]; "...that summer light, that luminous gloam, seeming bred especial for the *boreal* lands where Nature unveils her most beautiful soul, her most sacred countenance."
– Robin Devoe, *Overture: The Season of Light*

Borealism a fascination or inspiration derived from Earth's northern regions, esp. the Nordic countries and the Arctic; the concept can include ideas that the North is uniquely savage, barbaric, sublime, or pure; [inspired by the concept of Orientalism]

Borg Massif a group of mountains in eastern Antarctica

Boring Oregon town with sister city Dull, Scotland

born to the purple born and raised as royalty

bourasque a tempest or storm; [French *bourrasque* (squall, gust of wind)]

bovarism or **bovarysm** an unreal conception of oneself that dominates enough to cause behavioral change, esp. when the conception is idealized or glorified and leads to tragic personal conflict, very unusual behavior, or outstanding achievement; [from the title character of Flaubert's novel *Madame Bovary*]

brachiate to move by grasping hold of something (often a tree branch) and swinging forward to the next hold; [Latin *bracchium* arm]; "Early in life, Tarzan mastered the art of *brachiation*."

brank to prance; to caper; to toss the head, as a horse trying to spurn the bit

Brannock device common instrument used to measure shoe size first patented in 1925; [American Charles *Brannock*]

Bravo Sierra bullsh*t; [NATO phonetic alphabet]

brazen bull or **bull of Phalaris** a supposed life-size bronze bull heated until anyone inside died; an acoustic device converted interior screams into bull sounds; [Ancient Greece]

Bridge of the Gods a natural land bridge over the Columbia River near Cascade Locks, Oregon – formed by a large landslide circa 1100 CE and subsequently eroded by the river; also a man-made bridge nearby

brisance the violence of an explosion, explosiveness; the destructive effect of the energy from an explosion; high likelihood of explosion; [perhaps from Latin *brisa* (post-crushed grape refuse) or Irish *brissim* (I break)]

Brocken spectre or **mountain spectre** an atmospheric phenomenon consisting of the shadow of an observer (that appears larger than normal) cast onto clouds in the opposite direction of the sun – the shadow's head is often surrounded by rings of colored light; [from the *Brocken* (also known as the *Blocksberg*), the highest mountain in northern Germany]

brontide a sound like distant thunder caused by seismic effects; the sound of distant thunder – often a long, low rumble

brontomancy using thunder to predict the future; [Ancient Greek *brontê* thunder]

brontophobia fear of thunder storms; fear of thunder or lightning

Brosno Dragon a monster inhabiting Brosno Lake, western Russia; [Russian folklore]

Brotherhood of Eternal Love, The a prominent Californian psychedelic drug ring in the 60's and 70's – nicknamed the *Hippie Mafia*

brown study deep, melancholy reflections; a moody daydream; gloomy ruminations

brumal occurring in winter; wintry

Brumalia an ancient Roman festival during winter solstice honoring the god Saturn and the goddess Ceres; [Latin *winter festivals*]

brume fog, mist, or vapors; [adj. *brumous*]

Bucephalus Alexander the Great's horse that he won by wagering his father he could tame it; [Ancient Greek *bous* (ox) + *kephalē* (head)]

Bucksnort a small community in Hickman County, Tennessee

bumfodder toilet paper; official papers; [informal]

Burrow Mump a hill, with a ruined church atop, in the English county of Somerset

buttling acting as a butler; [present participle of *buttle*]

Byzantium an old name for Istanbul, Turkey – Constantinople was the intervening appellation; a dark shade of purple; [Latin]

C

cacafuego a person with a hot temper; one prone to bragging; [from the nickname of a Spanish galleon – literally: *fire-sh*tter*]

cairngorm smoky quartz; [from *Cairngorms*, a Scottish mountain range]

caisson a chest to hold ammunition or explosives; an enclosure used for underwater construction

Caledonia Roman name for Scotland; [Latin; poetic]
"O *Caledonia*! Stern and wild,
Meet nurse for a poetic child!" – Sir Walter Scott

calenture a fever or illness brought on by heat, usually in the tropics; a delirium during which sailors of yore pictured the sea as green meadows and wanted to leap overboard into them

calescent increasing in warmth; growing hot

Caliban a man having a savage, beastly nature; [a character in Shakespeare's *The Tempest*]

caliginous dim; obscure; dark; gloomy; misty; [archaic]; [French *caligineux* (obscure, misty)]

callomania self-delusions that one is extremely beautiful; having an inordinate love of beauty

Cambria the Latin name for Wales; [Welsh *Cymru*]

cameleopard or **camelopard** a giraffe; [Ancient Greek –
from having a long neck like a camel (*kámēlos*) and spots
like a leopard (*párdalis*)]

camellia a type of Asian shrub

candescent glowing hot; white-hot; luminous; incandescent

canorous melodious; musical; resonant; sweet-sounding

cantabile in a melodious, lyrical, flowing style, esp. in music

cantillate to chant or intone; [Italian *canto* song]

capripede satyr; a person or creature with goat feet

carfax place where four roads meet; a town's main
intersection; [Latin *quadrifurcus* (four-forked)]

carnassial adapted for eating flesh

Carpathian Ruthenia a historic region incl. parts of Ukraine,
Poland, and Slovakia; [from *Carpathian* Mountains and
Ruthenian people]

Carrington Event, the an 1859 geomagnetic storm likely
caused by a coronal mass ejection; resulting auroras
were bright enough to read by at night and visible from
the Caribbean; [British astronomer Richard *Carrington*]

cashiered discharged from service, esp. dishonorably;
[Old French *casser* (to break up)]

Caspian Hyrcanian mixed forests an ecoregion of lush
forest next to the Caspian Sea in Iran and Azerbaijan;
[ancient region of *Hyrcania* – from Old Persian *Verkâna*
(Wolf-land)]

catadromous moving from freshwater to saltwater
to spawn; opposite of anadromous

celadon pale green; [Latin *Celadon*, a warrior in Ovid's
Metamorphoses]

centipawn 1/100th of the value of a pawn – a queen is often
valued at 900 centipawns; [used in computer chess]

ceraunomancy supernaturally gaining information from, or
controlling, thunder or lightning;
[Greek *ceraunos* thunderbolt]

ceraunophobia or **keraunophobia** a fear of thunder or
thunderstorms

cerebrotonic designating or resembling a type of personality which is introverted, intellectual, shy, and emotionally restrained

cerulescent close to cerulean, or sky blue; light-blue

chalcenterous or **chalcenteric** having bowels of brass or bronze (figurative); very tough; [Ancient Greek *khalkós* (copper, bronze)]

champaign flat, open country; "Through Alpine vale or *champaign* wide" – Wordsworth

chantefable in medieval French literature, a story written in prose and verse; [French *chanter* (to sing) + *fable* (story)]

chanteuse a female singer, esp. a nightclub singer

chantepleure singing and crying that is simultaneous or alternates; a small hole in a wall for letting water pass

chaogenous (kay-OJ-en-us) that which originates from chaos, or is chaos-born

chartless unmapped; "We drift on a *chartless*, resistless sea. Let us sing when we can, and forget the rest." – Lovecraft

chasmophile someone who loves nooks and crannies; [adj. *chasmophilous*]

Chattertonian of or relating to English poet Thomas Chatterton, who committed suicide in 1770 at age 17 and to whom Keats dedicated *Endymion*; an admirer or imitator of Chatterton or the pretense of his archaic literary style; [adj. & noun]

cheiloproclitic being attracted to a person's lips

chiliad a group of 1,000; millennium; a period of 1000 years; "Breeding athwart the cascading *chiliads*
Of fast fading foreyears –
The pipings of glories long lost,
The still susurrant voice of distant dreaming seas,
Of empires faint along horizons far glimmering..."
– Robin Devoe, *Deeping Legends of a Purple Land*

chimeric like a *chimera* – a flame-spewing creature in Greek myth. with heads of goat and lion, a goat's body, and a serpent's tail; imaginary

chiminage a toll for passage through a forest;
[French *chemin* (path, road)]

chirk to enliven; to make or become cheerful; lively; in good
spirits; [verb & adj.]

chirm collective term for goldfinches; noise, esp. confused
noise, clamor, the hum of many voices, birdsong, etc.

chitterlings or **chitlins** boiled and fried pig intestine

choric relating to or resembling a chorus

chrematistic related to wealth, the science of wealth, or the
measurement of wealth in terms of money;
[Ancient Greek *khrêma* money]

chronotype the natural disposition of someone to be more
(or less) alert, productive, etc. depending on the time of
day; "Beyond night owl, his *chronotype* was almost
vampiric."

chrysalis the cocooned pupa of a moth or butterfly
undergoing metamorphosis; the cocoon itself

chryselephantine composed of, or adorned with, gold and
ivory; [Ancient Greek *khrusós* (gold) + *elephántinos*
(of ivory)]

Chrysopelea a genus of mildly venomous forest- or jungle-
dwelling flying snake endemic to Southeast Asia; nearly
doubles its width during glides of up to 100 meters

chrysophilist a lover of gold

chthonic (THON-uhk) of or relating to the earth or the
underworld; living under the earth; dark, primitive, and
mysterious

cimmerian (suh-MAIR-ree-uhn) dark and gloomy;
[from *Cimmerians* in Homer's *Odyssey*: a people
who lived in a land of everlasting night; the fictional
Conan the Barbarian was Cimmerian];
"Melt and dispel, ye spectre-doubts, that roll
Cimmerian darkness o'er the parting soul!"
– Thomas Campbell, 19th c. Scottish poet

Circean (SUR-see-un) like Circe; pleasing or enchanting, but
also depraving or debasing; [*Circe* in Homer's *Odyssey*

first charmed Odysseus's men, then turned them into animals]

circumbendibus circumlocution; an indirect manner of traveling, speaking, or writing

circumcrescent growing around, above, or over

circumfulgent shining around; [Latin *circum-* round]

circumfuse to pour around; to surround (with a fluid); suffuse

circumjacent bordering on every side; surrounding

circummure to encompass or surround with a wall

circumvolant flying around

circumzenithal arc an atmospheric phenomenon similar to an upside-down rainbow caused by refraction of sunlight through ice crystals

cirrus (pl. *cirri*) a cloud type composed of white, wispy, and delicate filaments; [Latin *cirrus* (curl, forelock)]; "Ale-colored sunshine and pale sky and whorls of *cirrus* so high they cast no shadow. Insects all business all the time. Quartz and chert and schist and chondrite iron scabs in granite. Very old land. Look around you. The horizon trembling, shapeless. We are all of us brothers." – David Foster Wallace, American author (1962-2008)

cisalpine on the south, or Roman, side of the Alps; [Latin *cis* (on this side of)]

cismontane this side of the mountains

City of Sails, The nickname for Auckland, NZ

City of the Caesars or **the Wandering City** a mythical Patagonian city set in an Andean valley between mountains of gold and diamond

clair de lune pale blue-gray; [French *moonlight*]

clapperclaw to claw with fingernails; to verbally abuse; to scold harshly; to cruelly toy with

cleftal horizon the transition zone between cheek and natal cleft on human buttocks

cloud cuckoo land imaginary land metaphorically inhabited by silly or unrealistic people; a state of absurd fantasy;

[the name of the bird-built city in Aristophanes' play
The Birds]

cloud-ridden full of clouds; obscured by clouds

cockshut evening; twilight; [obsolete];
"Mistress, this is only spite
For you would not yesternight
Kiss him in the *cock-shut* light."
– Ben Jonson, English playwright and poet, 1603

collachrymate to weep together; to commiserate;
[noun: *collachrymation*]; [Italian *lacrima* tear]

coloratura fancy or florid passages in vocal music, esp. trills
and brilliant runs, often used to display a singer's skill;
music containing same; [Italian *coloratura* (to color)]

Come By Chance a town on the Isthmus of Avalon in
Labrador & Newfoundland, Canada; also a town in
New South Wales, Australia

complot to plot a conspiracy together; to conspire; [archaic]

conglobe to form into a spherical shape; to make globular;
[poetic]

constellate to combine as a cluster; to unite as in a
constellation; "This most exquisite twilight of the boreal
half-night and all the sweet feelings that *constellate*
around it (including, it seems, some of the strongest and
noblest feelings of which humans are capable)..."
– Robin Devoe, *Overture: The Season of Light*

Copeland Septet a group of seven galaxies in the
constellation Leo discovered in 1874; [British
Astronomer Ralph *Copeland*]

Corona Borealis a seven-star constellation in the northern
celestial hemisphere and one of the 88 modern
constellations; [Latin *northern crown*]

corpuscles of Herbst nerve endings in certain parts
of birds, incl. the tongue's mucous membrane;
[German embryologist Curt Alfred *Herbst*]

corybantic wildly excited; frenzied; madly agitated;
[from the *Korybantes*, armored male dancers who

worshipped the mother goddess Cybele with drumming and dancing]; [Greek myth.]

cosmocrat or **kosmokrator** ruler or prince of the world; prosperous person living a global lifestyle

cosmogenesis the origin and development of the universe; [adj. *cosmogenic*]

cosmographic pertaining to the creation of maps of the universe; pertaining to the study of the universe's geometry

cosmoplastic pertaining to the formation of the world, esp. independently of God; world-forming

cosmopoietic referring to the creation of the cosmos or universe; world-producing

cosmopolite a world citizen; a cosmopolitan person; "The wild goose is more of a *cosmopolite* than we; he breaks his fast in Canada, takes a luncheon in the Ohio, and plumes himself for the night in a southern bayou." – Henry David Thoreau, *Walden*

cosmotron a type of particle accelerator

countenance a face, or an expression thereof; to give support or sanction to; to approve or tolerate; [noun & verb]

coup de soleil a sunstroke or other sun-induced malady; [French]

cragfast stranded on a crag or in a remote rocky area

crepuscular like or pertaining to twilight; glimmering; [Latin & English *crepusculum* twilight]; "*crepuscular* depths of personality"– William James

crescentic (adj.) growing; increasing; crescent-shaped

cri de coeur an impassioned outcry (as of appeal or protest); [French *cry from the heart*]

cribellum (pl. *cribella*) an organ with many fine pores used for spinning silk in some spiders

criosphinx a sphinx with the head of a ram; [Greek *krios* ram]

Croesus a person of great wealth; [a rich king of ancient Lydia – now western Turkey]; "...an intellectual *Croesus*..." – Henry James

cryptogenic of uncertain or unknown origin, esp. a *cryptogenic* species

crystallomancy using crystal to foretell the future

Cthulhu large, alien, Lovecraftian god with a head resembling an octopus and dragon-like wings; [adj. *Cthulhuesque*]; "...bolder than the storied Cyclops, great *Cthulhu* slid greasily into the water and began to pursue with vast wave-raising strokes of cosmic potency." – H. P. Lovecraft

cummingtonite a type of mineral first identified in the small town of Cummington, Massachusetts

cupreous the color of polished copper; containing copper; copper-like; [Latin]

curglaff the shock of suddenly jumping into cold water; [Scottish]

cuspate foreland a triangular geographic feature extending outward from a waterbody's shoreline

cwm (koom) a steep, glacially formed valley roughly shaped like an amphitheater; a cirque; [Welsh]

cwtch a hiding place; a cubbyhole; a cuddle or hug; [Welsh]

cyanometer instrument for measuring degrees of blueness, esp. of the sky or ocean

Cygnus a constellation in the Northern Hemisphere AKA the Northern Cross or the Swan; Cygnus contains the star Deneb – a very bright star in the Summer Triangle

Cytherean pertaining to the goddess Aphrodite or Venus, thus also pertaining to beauty; pertaining to the planet Venus; Venusian; [from *Cythera*, the island where Aphrodite came ashore on a seashell in Greek myth.]

D

daedal having an ingenious or complex design; finely or skillfully created; artistic; [adj. *daedalian*];

"...The *daedal* earth,
That island in the ocean of the world,
Hung in its cloud of all-sustaining air."
  – Shelley, *Ode to Liberty*

Dali a beautiful goddess of the hunt, with golden hair and glowing skin, who lived in a cavern at the side of an alpine glacier; also referred to as Dali of the Rocks, the Mistress of Beasts, or Angel of the Crags; [Georgian myth.]

Damaraland a historic political region located in what is now Namibia in Southwest Africa

Damascene moment when an epiphany leads to a decisive turning point in one's life, like what happened to Apostle Paul on the road to Damascus

damoiseau (dam-wah-zoo) a young male of noble birth who has yet to become a knight; a young noble escort; masculine counterpart of the word *damsel*; [French]

dangerman a player on an opposing sports team who poses a significant threat

dapatical sumptuous; expensive; [Latin *daps* feast]; [obsolete]

Daphnean shy and beautiful; of or pertaining to *Daphne*, a dryad pursued by Apollo; [Greek myth.]

dark flow in astrophysics, a theoretical component of the relative velocity of galaxy clusters

darkle to grow or make dark;
"The air grows cool and *darkles,*
The Rhine flows calmly on;
The mountain summit sparkles
In the light of the setting sun."
  – Heinrich Heine, German Romantic poet

Dark Side of the Rainbow pairing Pink Floyd's album *Dark Side of the Moon* with the 1939 film *The Wizard of Oz* to produce striking moments where the two appear to correspond

darshan an audience with a spiritual leader; euphoria, grace, or blessedness derived from same; [Sanskrit *darśana* vision]

daven to pray, esp. to recite the Jewish liturgy; [present participle: *davening*]

declivity a downward slope, esp. a steep one; [adj. *declivitous*]; "Routine is a *declivity* down which many governments slide, and routine says that freedom of the press is dangerous." – José Rizal 19th c. Filipino nationalist

deipnosophist someone possessing great skill in dining and dining room conversation; [Ancient Greek *deîpnon* meal]

deliquesce to melt away or to appear to melt into nothing; [adj. *deliquescent*]

Delmarva peninsula on America's East Coast containing parts of three states, incl. most of Delaware; [a clipped compound of **Del**aware, **Mar**yland, and **V**irgini**a**]

Delphic or **Delphian** of or relating to Delphi, or to the famous oracle of Delphi; often lowercase: ambiguous; mysterious; prophetic; brotherly;
"Such graves as his are pilgrim shrines,
Shrines to no code or creed confined,—
The *Delphian* vales, the Palestines,
The Meccas of the mind."
– Fitz-Greene Halleck, 19th c. American poet

démarche (DAY-marsh) a decisive or well-finessed diplomatic action, esp. one starting a new policy; [French]

demersal sinking to the bottom of the sea; subaqueous; living underwater or near the seabed; [Latin *demersus* sunk]

demimonde a class of women kept by wealthy lovers or protectors; women prostitutes considered as a group; mistress; [French, literally: *half-world*]

demiurge God, as maker of the world; something that is an autonomous creative force; [adj. *demiurgic*]

demulcent softening; mollifying; soothing; assuasive

dendrophile a lover of trees or forests

desideratum (pl. *desiderata*) that which is desired; any improvement which is wanted; [Latin]

desiderium (pl. *desideria*) a fervent desire, esp. for something formerly possessed and now missed; emotional pain from missing something or someone; [Latin]; [adj. & verb: *desiderate*]

desuetude the cessation of use; disuse; inactivity; [French]; "The specialty factories florished, while the very populace itself – curiously consumed by wealth – into decadent asyla of *desuetude* fell."

de trop superfluous; excessive; unwanted, esp. related to a person's presence; [French *of too much*]

devaloka in Indic religions, a plane of existence home to gods & devas (god-like celestial beings)

devenustate to deprive of beauty or grace; to disfigure; [Latin *venustus* (lovely, graceful)]

Devi a Hindu goddess; the embodiment of the female energy of Shiva and having both beneficent and malevolent forms; [Sanskrit]

Devonian a geologic period (between the Silurian and the Carboniferous), during part of which extensive forests covered the continents; [from *Devon*, England]

dianoetic pertaining to thought or to the use of reason rather than intuition

digerati collectively, people who are considered the elite (for whatever reason) in information technology; [digital + literati]

dionysian uninhibited; spontaneous; wild; orgiastic; [*Dionysus*, the god of wine and fertility in Greek myth.]

Diogenic or **diogenic** like the Greek philosopher Diogenes; cynical

discompose to disturb; to agitate from a calm state; to create disorder; "I am glad I have done being in love with him. I should not like a man who is so soon *discomposed* by a hot morning."
– Jane Austen, English novelist (1775-1817)

displume to remove the feathers of; to strip of honors or of an award; "Within a year of being so ignominiously *displumed*, the professor published his greatest work."

distillate the liquid condensed from vapor during distillation, usually in a purified form; the essense of something

dithyrambic pertaining to or resembling a dithyramb (in ancient Greek poetry, a hymn in honor of Bacchus, full of transport and poetical rage); wild and boisterous; very enthusiastic; wild and emotional speech or writing; [adj. & noun]

divagate to wander about or meander; to stray from a subject, focus, or course; [Latin *vagus* roaming]

dolce far niente the pure enjoyment of being idle, lazy, or relaxed; [noun]; [Italian *sweet idleness*]

Don Juan Pond a shallow, Antarctic hypersaline lake that stays liquid down to -50 °C; [from two helicopter pilots named *Don* and *John*]

doodlesack bagpipes – a Scottish, woodwind musical instrument; [archaic]

Doom Mons a probable *cryovolcano* on Titan, the largest moon of Saturn

doomscrolling or **doomsurfing** obsessively or continually reading bad news, esp. Internet news (or related social media posts) on catastrophes

Dorking an English town 21 miles south of London

double-barrelled surnames a hyphenated or otherwise combined surname common in various traditions

drachenfutter a gift offered as appeasement to a romantic partner who is upset; [German, literally: *dragon fodder*]; "After measuring the pub's remaining pleasures against the bother of finding *drachenfutter* to sooth a partner easily discomposed, he quickly made for home."

draconic suggestive of a dragon; draconian; very strict, cruel, or severe

Dragonfish Nebula a large nebula discovered in 2010; [resembles the deep-sea *dragonfish*]

dragonnade a rapid and devastating military incursion or persecution

Dragon's Blood Forest unique dragon blood trees growing on the Yemeni island of Socotra in the Arabian Sea and producing a red sap

drake a male duck

Drakensburg the eastern portion of the Great Escarpment, a highland area in southern Africa; [Dutch *Drakensbergen* (Dragons' Mountains)]

drakestone a flat stone used for skipping on water

dreadnaught or **dreadnought** a thick woolen coat; a large battleship with many powerful guns; British class of ship made in 1906; something the largest or most powerful of its class; [*dread + nought* – fear nothing]

dreamfish any of several species of fish the eating of which may produce hallucinations, esp. *Sarpa salpa*

droog a gang member, esp. one young and violent; [from the novel *A Clockwork Orange*]; [Russian *drug* friend]; [adj. *droogish*]

drosometer a device used to measure the weight of dew on a surface; [Ancient Greek *drósos* dew]

Dr. Strangelove someone who is irresponsible and rash with dangerous weapons, esp. nuclear bombs; [from the 1964 British-American black comedy film *Dr. Strangelove*]; [adj. *Strangelovian*]

dryad female tree spirit; woodnymph; [Greek myth.];
"...thou, light-winged *Dryad* of the trees,
  In some melodious plot
Of beechen green, and shadows numberless,
  Singest of summer in full-throated ease."
  – John Keats, *Ode to a Nightingale*

dulcifluous flowing sweetly

dulciloquent speaking in a sweet or charming way

dwaal a dreamy or befuddled state of mind; [Afrikaans]

E

earthdrake a dragon-like beast; [Anglo-Saxon myth.]

Earth-grazing fireball a very bright meteor that enters the Earth's atmosphere but survives to reenter outer space with an altered orbit

Earthshine or **the Moon's ashen glow** the dim reflected glow on the portion of the Moon's face not directly illuminated by the sun; from sunlight reflected by the earth's surface & clouds

Eastern Question the political and diplomatic issues raised by the waning power of the Ottoman Empire; the Russo-Turkish war (1828-29) first brought these issues to the fore, esp. for Russia and Britain; "To the *Eastern Question*, the Dual Alliance had a northern answer."

Echo a nymph who, spurned by Narcissus, pined away until only her voice remained; [Greek myth.]

edgelord someone attempting to sound edgy by saying something offensive; [slang]

eidolon an image or representation; a form; a phantom; an apparition; "By a route obscure and lonely,
Haunted by ill angels only,
Where an *Eidolon*, named Night,
On a black throne reigns upright,
I have reached these lands but newly
From an ultimate dim Thule..." – Edgar Allan Poe

eldren or **eldern** old; ancient

elephant bird family of birds in Madagascar extinct since 1200 CE – the largest species stood 10 feet tall, weighed 1600 pounds, and laid 22-pound eggs about 160 times larger than chicken eggs

El Gordo a particularly large and distant galaxy cluster; [Spanish *the big one*]

Eliotic or **Eliotian** of or like the style of poet T. S. Eliot; "The Kiplingesque grandeur of Waterloo Station, the *Eliotic* despondency of the brick row in Chelsea ... the

Dickensian nightmare of fog and sweating pavement and besmirched cornices." – John Updike, American novelist

eluvium (pl. *eluviums* or *eluvia*) in geology, deposits of rock, dust, and soil particles left by wind action; [adj. *eluvial*]

elver a young eel

Elysian of or relating to Elysium; blissful; heavenly;
"They know not of the poetry which lies
Upon the summer rose's languid eyes;
They have no spiritual visitings *elysian*,
They dream no dreamings, and they see no vision."
– Letitia E. Landon, 19th c. English poet

Elysium or **Elysian Fields** in Greek myth., home of the blessed after death; paradise;
"Joy, beautiful spark of Divinity,
Daughter of *Elysium*,
We enter, drunk with fire,
Heavenly one, thy sanctuary!"
– 18th c. German poet Friedrich Schiller, *Ode to Joy*

embonpoint plumpness, esp. when voluptuous; [French];
"The beautiful woman threw off her sabletrimmed wrap, displaying her queenly shoulders and heaving *embonpoint*." – James Joyce, 20th c. Irish novelist

embuggerance any hazard or obstacle, whether natural or artificial, that impedes or complicates a proposed course of action; [British military slang]

empanoply to enclose completely in armor;
"The grand conglomerate hills of Araby,
That stand *empanoplied* in utmost thought,
With dazzling ramparts front the Indian sea,
Down there in Hadramaut."
– Bayard Taylor, 19th c. American poet & diplomat

Emperor Seamounts a Pacific Ocean mountain range, mostly undersea, that includes the Hawaiian Islands – the highest point is Mauna Kea which has a *dry prominence* (5125m below sea level plus 4205m above) second only to Mount Everest

emprise an enterprise, endeavor, or adventure; the
   qualities which prompt one to undertake difficult
   and dangerous exploits;
   "In brave pursuit of chivalrous *emprise*."– Spenser;
   "I love thy courage yet, and bold *Emprise*,
   But here thy sword can do thee little stead." – Milton

Empty Quarter the world's largest sand desert, covering the
   southern third of the Arabian Peninsula and parts of four
   countries: Saudi Arabia, Yemen, UAE, and Oman

empurple to tinge or dye a purple color; to discolor with
   purple; "He tasted the bright sting of the pugilist's
   empurpling fist."

empyreal formed of pure fire or light; pertaining to the
   highest and purest region of heaven; pure; vital; celestial;
   elevated; "Go, soar with Plato to th'*empyreal* sphere..."
   – Alexander Pope, 18th c. English poet

empyrean the highest region of Heaven; the home of God;
   paradise; the sky; belonging to heaven; [noun & adj.];
   "Lispings *empyrean* will I sometime teach
   thine honied tongue..." – John Keats, *Endymion*

Endymion in Greek myth., a beautiful youth cast into
   eternal sleep by Zeus and loved by Selene, goddess of
   the Moon; "How many things by season season'd are
   To their right praise, and true perfection! –
   Peace, ho! the moon sleeps with *Endymion*,
   And would not be awak'd!"
   – Shakespeare, *The Merchant of Venice*

engraft to graft together one plant with another; to
   establish or set firmly and securely; to implant

engrailment a ring of dots or notches around the edge
   of a coin or a medal

ensanguine to stain with blood

ensorcell or **ensorcel** to bewitch or enchant someone;
   "Every rift of that boreal dream's blue midnight, her
   ensorcelling charm infused..."

entheogen a psychoactive substance used to induce an experience that is seemingly mystical or that supposedly develops one's spirituality; [Ancient Greek *éntheos* (full of the god, inspired) + *genésthai* (to come into being)]

enubilous free from fog, mist, or clouds; clear; [poetic]; [verb: *enubilate*]

envermeil to color red or vermilion

ephemeron (pl. *ephemera*) something that is short-lived or transitory; [adj. *ephemeral*]

epichorial in or of a rural area or the countryside; "...*epichorial* superstitions from every district of Europe..." – Thomas De Quincey

epsilon axe a type of ancient bronze or copper battle axe originating in the Middle East; [named for similarity to the Greek letter *epsilon*]

equilibrist a tightrope walker; [archaic]

equipluve a line on a map showing equal amounts of rainfall

equipollent having equal power; equivalent

equiponderous having equal weight

equivoque a pun or double-meaning; an *equivocal* expression; [obsolete]

Erdős-Bacon number the sum of one's degree of separation from authoring an academic paper with Hungarian mathematician Paul *Erdős* and being in a film with American actor Kevin *Bacon* – two mathematicians have numbers of 3 due to co-authoring papers with Erdős and being in films with actors who were in films with Bacon

Erin Ireland; [Irish *Éirinn*]; [poetic]

erinaceous like or pertaining to a hedgehog

erlking in German myth., a malevolent elf or spirit that esp. plagues children; [German *Erlkönig* (alder-king)]

esper a person or being possessing paranormal abilities or advanced mental capabilities; [*ESP* (extrasensory perception) + *er*]

esperance hope; expectation;
   "Sith yet there is a credence in my heart,
   An *esperance* so obstinately strong,
   That doth invert the attest of eyes and ears..."
   – Shakespeare, *Troilus and Cressida*
Esperance a town on the Southern Ocean in Australia;
   [from a French ship, the *Espérance*]
espiègle playful; frolicsome; roguish; mischievous; [French]
esprit d'escalier the feeling one gets when thinking of
   things one should have said too late, after exiting a
   conversation; afterwit; such a remark itself;
   [French, literally: *mind of the staircase*]
Esquiline one of the seven hills of Rome
euphorigenic of or pertaining to causing euphoria
Europa a princess of Phoenicia (modern Lebanon) who was
   abducted by Zeus (in the form of a white bull) and taken
   to Crete, where she reigned as Queen; also a moon of
   Jupiter; [Greek myth.]
evanish to vanish; to disappear; to escape from sight or
   perception; [archaic];
   "Or like the rainbow's lovely form,
   Evanishing amid the storm." – Robert Burns, Scottish poet
eviternity eternity; eternal existence
excandescent red or white-hot; glowing with heat
excreta (pl. only) human waste excreted from the body
exothermic releasing heat; [chemistry]
expatiate to elaborate at length in speech or writing;
   to range at large, or without restraint
exsibilation the disapproving hisses of an audience
extraforaneous pertaining to things out of doors; outdoor;
   [Latin *foras* (out of doors)]; [archaic]

F

fanfarade fanfare; a flourish of trumpets; a showy display
fantastico a very strange or bizarre person; [Italian]
farblondjet lost; confused; [Yiddish *completely lost*]

fata morgana a mirage caused by temperature inversion where distant objects are distorted, often appearing to float in air – esp. such a mirage in the Strait of Messina, between Italy and Sicily; [Italian; from the Arthurian sorceress *Morgan le Fay*]

favonian pertaining to the west wind; soft; mild; gentle; [Latin *favonius* (the west wind)]

Feathered Serpent, the a supernatural entity found in several Mesoamerican religions

febricity feverishness; [adj. *febrile*]; [Latin *febris* fever]

fellmonger a seller of animal hides or skins; [British]

felsenmeer an area covered with angular boulders broken up by the freeze and thaw cycle – occurring in mountainous Arctic regions on slopes less than 25 degrees; [German *sea of rock*]

femtosecond one quadrillionth part of a second; 1/1000th of a picosecond; [Danish *femten* fifteen]

Fennoscandia peninsula including the mainlands of Norway, Sweden, and Finland, and part of Russia; [Latin *Fennia* (Finland) + *Scandia* (Scandinavia)]

ferly strange; exceptional; causing wonder; terror-inducing; [Scots]

fern flower in Baltic myth., a magic flower bringing good fortune that blooms for a single night during summer solstice; [Latvian *papardes zieds* (fern flower)]

fernbrake a patch of ferns; [*bracken* – area with many ferns]

Feronia a goddess of fertility, wildlife, and abundance; [Roman myth.]

fey magical or fairy-like; strange or otherworldly; fated to die; doomed; overrefined; quaint

fictive fictitious; imaginary; feigned; counterfeit; "the fount of *fictive* tears" – Alfred, Lord Tennyson

Fiddler's Green a legendary afterlife – for sailors who served at least 50 years asea – consisting of constant fiddle music, dancers who never tire, and eternal mirth; any pleasant place where sailors may frolic ashore

filipendulous suspended by a single thread; [Latin *filum* (thread) + *pendulus* (hanging)]

Fimbulheimen an Antarctic mountain range

Fimbulwinter in Norse myth., a three-year winter that kills all life, except two humans, and is followed by Ragnarök (natural disasters and wars); [Old Norse *fimbulvetr* (the great winter)]

Fin de siècle pertaining to the end of any century, but esp. the 19th century when feelings of world-weariness and self-indulgence seemed to pervade the literary and artistic world; the end of any era; [adj. & noun]; [French *end of century*]

fingersmith a pick pocket; [archaic]

firedrake a fire-breathing dragon; a furnace worker; a meteor; "...wishes cast upon *firedrake* fallen."

firmament the sky; the heavens;
"Now glowed the *firmament*
With living sapphires; Hesperus, that led
The starry host, rode brightest..."
– John Milton, *Paradise Lost*

First East Turkestan Republic from 1934-35, an Islamic republic centered around Kashgar in present-day Xinjiang, western China – largely founded by Uyghur peoples

fissilingual having a forked or cleft tongue; [Latin *fissus* split]

Five Flavored Tea of Forgetfulness a brew, the drinking of which erases all memory of one's past lives; [Chinese myth.]

fjeld high plateau in Scandinavia

flail threshing tool used to harvest grain; an ancient weapon consisting of a handle, an often spherical and spiked striking part, and a connecting chain;

Flaming Teeth a giant with very large teeth appearing as burning logs – its killing led to man's first use of fire; [Fijian myth.]

flammagenitus or **pyrocumulus cloud** a dense cumuliform cloud created by forest fire or volcanic eruption

flammivomous vomiting or expelling flames, like a volcano; [poetic]

flashover the near simultaneous combustion of material in an enclosed area

flocculent spiral galaxy a type of galaxy with discontinuous spiral arms

floramour old name for *amaranthus caudatus* – a tropical, partially edible, reddish-flowered plant with common names including love-lies-bleeding, pendant amaranth, and velvet flower

floricomous having one's hair or head decorated with flowers; [Latin *floris* (flower) + *coma* (hair)]

flumadiddle utter nonsense; worthless frills

Flumserberg a ski resort area in the Swiss Alps

flying dragon or **gliding lizard** Asian lizards of the genus *Draco* – capable of gliding 200 feet

foehn (fayn) warm, dry wind blowing down a mountainside, esp. in the Alps; [German *Föhn*]

foredeep in geology, a deep depression on the seafloor offshore a mountainous area

foregleam an antecedent or premonitory gleam; a glimpse of the future; a dawning light

fore-night time between twilight and going to bed

foreshots the first liquid to issue from a still

forfend to forbid; to prohibit; to avert

forjeskit weary and jaded; [Scottish]

Formosan clouded leopard extinct Taiwanese leopard

Fornax a constellation in the southern celestial hemisphere; [Latin *furnace*]

foudroyant thunderous; noisy; dazzling; overwhelming or stunning in effect; [French, from Latin *fulgur* (lightning)]

foxfire bioluminescence from a fungus that grows on decaying wood

frabjous fabulous; joyous; great; wonderful;
"O *frabjous* day! Callooh! Callay!
He chortled in his joy."
– Lewis Carroll, *Jabberwocky*

freebooter one who plunders or pillages without the
authority of national warfare; a member of a predatory
band; a pillager; a buccaneer; a sea robber; a pirate;
[*free+booty+er*]

freemartin a sterile female calf, born with a bull twin;
an infertile woman; [last meaning rare]

freighted burdened; loaded; "Ocean is more ancient than
the mountains, and *freighted* with the memories and the
dreams of Time." – Lovecraft

Fremantle Doctor cool afternoon sea breeze;
[*Fremantle* – a town near Perth, Australia]

fremescence the sound of a crowd of people trending
toward displeasure

fremescent rumbling; very noisy or riotous; starting to roar

Freyja or **Freya** Celtic goddess associated with love, beauty,
sex, war, and gold; lynxes drew her chariot and she wore
a cloak of falcon feathers

frisson a sudden surge of excitement; a shiver;
[Old French *fricon* (a trembling)]

fritinancy the chirping or croaking of insects

frostwork any intricate pattern of ice crystals; something
resembling such a pattern

frottage the practice of two consenting humans, usually
clothed, rubbing body parts together for sexual
stimulation; [French]

F*ckersberg a town in northern Austria, pop. 21

fugleman (pl. *fuglemen*) one who leads a group or a
company, esp. in military exercises; a political leader;
[German]

fulgent radiant; shining brightly; "And universally, the
greatest and most *fulgent* tails always arise from Comets,
immediately after their passing..." – Sir Isaac Newton, 1729

fulgurous or **fulgurant** resembling lightning; impressive like a series of lightning flashes; [Latin *fulgur* lightning]

fulmen lightning; thunderbolt; [Latin]

fulminate to cause to explode or detonate; to strike with (or as if with) lightning; to launch a verbal attack; to make a thundering or loud noise; [adj. & noun: *fulminant*]

fumiferous producing smoke

G

galactic tide the tidal force exerted on objects subject to the gravitational field of a galaxy

galactic year the time it takes for our solar system to revolve around the center of the galaxy – 250 million years; the Earth is about 20 galactic years old

galaxy quenching a process during which a galaxy loses cold gas, greatly suppressing the formation of new stars

gallery forest trees growing along a riverbank in an otherwise forestless area – often dense and without understory

gallinipper a large mosquito; any large, biting insect; a giant mosquito – fabled creature from African-American folklore

gallivant or **galavant** to wander around searching for pleasure; to flirt

gammerstang a tall and awkward human, esp. a female; [British; archaic]

Gasherbrum II the 13th highest mountain in the world – located on the Chinese-Pakistani border in the Karakoram mountain range

Gates of Alexander or the **Caspian Gates** a barrier supposedly built by Alexander the Great at a pass in the Caucasus Mountains between Georgia and Russia

gaucherie an awkward or socially unacceptable action or remark; clumsiness; boorishness; [French]; "This club has endured your *gaucheries* for far too long!"

gaywings perennial flowering plant with white and pink flowers; "My moon and stars, how if I proffer these *gaywings* – is now your heart mended?"

gazingstock a spectacle; something that causes many people to look; [archaic]

gegenschein a faint brightening visible in the night sky's antisolar point (area furthest from the sun) caused by interplanetary dust backscattering sunlight; counterglow; [German *countershine*]

gelogenic causing laughter; [Ancient Greek *gélōs* laughter]

gemutlich having an atmosphere of amiability; friendly and pleasant; [German]

genetrix a mother; a female ancestor or progenitor

georgic (jor-jick) relating to agriculture or rural affairs; a poem relating to same; rural; pastoral; "Long he bathed in the *georgic* mansuetude of that alpestrine aestivation."

ghosten pertaining to ghosts; ghostly; to make ghost-like; [adj. & verb]; [poetic]; "The moon-*ghostened* trees shimmering skyward seemed to complete the lovely, yet eldritch scene."

gibber a boulder; to speak rapidly and inarticulately; to prattle; "The graves stood tenantless, and the sheeted dead / Did squeak and *gibber* in the Roman streets;" – Shakespeare, *Hamlet*

Gilded Age, the American era roughly from the Civil War's end until 1900 – noted for rapid economic expansion, corruption, and limited regulation; [*gilded* because serious social problems were figuratively overlaid with a thin layer of the "gold" of economic expansion]

gill a mountain stream; [English Lake District]

Gilliamesque akin to the works of British film director Terry Gilliam; fantastical, wildly imaginative, or surreal

ginch, gitch, gotch, or **gonch** underwear, esp. men's tighty-whities; [western Canadian slang]; "Yo, zude, your *ginch* be showing, eh?"

Gjallarhorn in Norse myth., a horn the god Heimdallr uses
to drink from the well of wisdom – the horn can be
heard in all Nine Worlds; [Old Norse *loud-sounding horn*]

glabrescent lacking hair, losing hair, or becoming hairless

glacier mouse a ball of moss sometimes found on glaciers

Glasir in Norse myth., a very beautiful tree (or grove)
with red gold leaves outside Valhalla in Asgard;
[Old Norse *gleaming*]

gleed a live or glowing coal; [Scots *gleed* ember]

gleefreshing or **joyscrolling** obsessively reading good
news, esp. good Internet news following a major, positive
event; [*glee + refreshing*]

glim a light; a glimpse; to shine; [noun & verb]; [archaic]

Glimfeather name of a large, white owl in the C. S. Lewis
novel *The Silver Chair*

glimflashy angry; [archaic]

glisk a glimpse; a gleam of light; [Scottish]

glissade to slide, sitting or standing, down a snow or
ice-covered slope; a move in dance and ballet; [French]

glister to gleam; to sparkle; [adj. *glistering*]
"All that *glisters* is not gold."
– Shakespeare, *The Merchant of Venice*
"'Tis better to be lowly born,
And range with humble livers in content,
Than to be perk'd up in a *glistering* grief,
And wear a golden sorrow."
– Shakespeare, *Henry VIII*

glitterati the rich and famous; stylish celebrities; highly
fashionable people prominent in the public eye;
[*glitter + literati*]

gloaming twilight; dusk;
"The *gloaming* comes, the day is spent,
The sun goes out of sight,
And painted is the Occident
With purple sanguine bright."
– Alexander Hume, 16th c. Scottish poet

Globus aerostaticus an obsolete constellation conceived by a French astronomer to honor the Montgolfier brothers' invention; [Latin *hot air balloon*]

gloomleader someone who promotes worst case scenarios; someone who actively spreads pessimism

glossolalia speaking in a language one has never learned; speaking in tongues

glottis (pl. *glottides*) the narrow opening between the true vocal cords; the vocal apparatus of the larynx

gobbet a lump or chunk, esp. of raw meat; an extract of text or image, esp. a quotation provided as context for analysis, translation, or discussion in an examination

Godolphin Arabian an Arabian stallion born in 1724 and one of three to sire the modern Thoroughbred racing line; [Francis *Godolphin*, 2nd Earl of *Godolphin*]

goetic (go-etik) of or pertaining to witchcraft, black magic, or necromancy; [Ancient Greek *goēteía* witchcraft]

Golden Dawn, the a secret society founded by Freemasons and focused on spiritual development through the practise & study of the occult, paranormality, and metaphysics; in 1888 the group opened the *Isis-Urania Temple* in London

golden fairy lantern a type of lily with yellow flowers that grows in northern California

Golden Horde a Mongol khanate originating as part of the Mongol Empire – invaded eastern Europe in the 13th c.

Gondwanaland the southern supercontinent formed after Pangaea's break up and before the Triassic period; [Sanskrit *goṇḍavana* (Forest of Gondi)]

gorcock the moorcock; red grouse

Gordian Knot a very complex problem, requiring somewhat transcendent, bold, or unorthodox means to solve; an intricate knot tied by Gordius, King of Phrygia – an oracle foretold that whoever untied the knot would be ruler of Asia: Alexander the Great simply cut it with his sword; [Gordium is Latin for *Gordion*, capital of Phrygia, an ancient kingdom located within modern-day Turkey]

gorgonize to have the effect of a Gorgon upon; to turn to stone; to petrify; [after *Gorgon*, any of the three monstrous sisters Stheno, Euryale, or Medusa in Greek myth. who could turn to stone anyone making eye contact]

gormless dull or stupid; lacking intelligence or discernment; inexperienced; very naive; [British]; [Old Norse *gaum* (heed, attention)]

götterdämmerung in Germanic myth., the destruction of the gods in a final battle with evil forces; any cataclysmic downfall, esp. of a regime or an institution; [German *Götterdämmerung* (twilight of the gods)]

goy (pl. *goyim*) a non-Jewish person; [Yiddish]

grandeval ancient; very old; [Latin *grandis* (great) + *aevum* (age)]

graustark an imaginary place of idealized adventure and romance; a piece of writing that includes idealized, romantic elements; [adj. *graustarkian*]; [from the imaginary country in Eastern Europe in the 1901 novel *Graustark*]

gravida a pregnant woman; [referred to as *gravida one* during first pregnancy, *gravida two* during the second, etc.]; [from Latin *gravis* heavy]

greking the dawn; [British]; [Old Norse *grýja* dawn]

griffin or **griffon** or **gryphon** a fabled beast with the head and wings of an eagle and a lion's body

griffonage bad handwriting, esp. when illegible; cacography; "One almost needs the Enigma machine to decipher his *griffonage*."

grike a crack separating blocks of limestone

grimoire (grim-wahr) an instruction book for casting magic spells, esp. black magic or sorcery; [French]

groak to look at longingly, esp. at someone eating while hoping for an offering

grok to have a complete intuitive understanding of something; [from the Martian word "to drink" and figuratively "to drink in all available aspects of reality" in Heinlein's *Stranger in a Strange Land*]

Groombridge 1830 a yellow-hued, subdwarf star 20 light years distant; [British astronomer Stephen *Groombridge*]

grootslang a legendary South African creature with an elephant's head and a snake's body – it feeds on elephants and hoards gems, esp. diamonds; [Dutch *big snake*]

gruntle a snort; a sound like grunting; to cause someone to be the opposite of disgruntled; [last meaning humorous slang]; "I could see that, if not actually disgruntled, he was far from being *gruntled*." – P.G. Wodehouse

gutbucket an early type of jazz/blues

guttler one who guttles, or eats voraciously; a glutton; [obsolete]

gyrovague a wondering monk with no home monastery; [Late Latin *gyro-* (circle) + *vagus* (wandering)]

H

halāhala a poison created when the sea was churned to create *amrita*, the nectar of immortality – to save other gods, Shiva drank the poison, turning his neck blue; [Hindu myth.]

halidom holiness; sanctity; sacred oath; sacred things; sanctuary

hamadryad in Greek & Roman myth., a type of wood nymph whose life ended when the particular tree she inhabited, usually an oak, died; [Ancient Greek *háma* (together) + *drûs* (tree)]

Hammerfest Norwegian town – northernmost settlement of over 5000 people in the world; [Old Norse *hamarr* (steep mountainside) + *festr* (fastening)]

hammerspace a storage space capable of storing things larger than itself; [from the large mallets some cartoon characters brandish from out of thin air]

Hanseatic League a commercial and military alliance of merchant guilds and market towns that controlled trade along northern European coasts from roughly the 12th to 17th centuries; [Old High German *hansa* (group or guild)]

Happy Adventure a coastal village in NE Canada

haptic relating to or based on the sense of touch; tactile; [Greek *haptesthai* (to touch)]

harmattan a dry, hot wind, prevailing on the Atlantic coast of Africa, blowing from the interior or the Sahara; [Arabic *haram* (forbidden thing)]

hegira an exodus or journey from a hostile or dangerous environment; [from the flight of Muhammad from Mecca to Medina in 622]

Helios god and personification of the sun and son of Hyperion; also the god of sight; [Greek myth.]

hellbender a species of giant salamander

helm wind a strong northeasterly wind in Cumbria, England

Helmi Stream a stellar stream (grouping of stars moving together) once a dwarf galaxy and now absorbed by the Milky Way; [Argentine astronomer Anima *Helmi*]

Helvetia Latin name for the pre-Roman Celtic country in the area that is now Switzerland

Helvetian Swiss; [poetic]

hemiboreal a climate between boreal (subarctic) and temperate, like much of southern Canada

hemicycle a half circle or semicircle; a place so shaped

hemipenis one of the two reproductive organs of male lizards and snakes

heptachord a seven-stringed musical instrument; a musical scale that has seven notes

Hesperia ancient Greek and Roman name for the Iberian Peninsula

Hesperian western; occidental; denoting or characteristic of Europe or the Western Hemisphere; relating to the land where the sun sets; "...the parting Sun

Beyond the Earth's green Cape and verdant Isles
Hesperian sets..." – John Milton, 17th c. English poet

Hesperides the nymphs of the golden light of setting suns
who tend a blissful orchard producing golden apples in
the far western corner of the world, near the Atlas
mountains at the edge of the world-ocean; [Greek myth.]

Hesperus Venus, when she is the evening star;
[Roman myth.]; [Ancient Greek *hésperos* western]

hesternal pertaining to yesterday; [Latin *hesternus*]

hibernacle that which serves for protection or shelter in
winter; winter living quarters for human, animal, or plant

Hibernia poetic name for Ireland; [Latin]

hiemal or **hibernal** belonging or relating to winter; wintry

higgler a peddler; an itinerant seller of small items;
one who haggles

Himmelreich a German town; [*kingdom of heaven*]

hindberry the raspberry; [archaic]

hinderlings the buttocks; [archaic]

hippogriff or **hippogryph** an imaginary creature, half-
horse and half-griffon (body of a lion with the wings &
head of an eagle); a winged horse;
"Saddle the *Hippogriffs*, ye Muses nine,
And straight we'll ride to the land of old Romance."
– Christoph Martin Wieland, 18th c. German poet

Hoder the blind Norse god who, tricked by Loki, unwittingly
killed his brother *Baldr* with a spear of mistletoe;
[Norse Myth.]

holmgang in Norse culture a duel, esp. one to the death;
[Old Norse *hólmganga* (island walk)]

honeyfuggle to swindle; [America; informal]

horizontal gluteal crease or **gluteal sulcus**
the horizontal crease between buttocks and thigh;
[Latin *sulcus* (a furrow made by a plow)]

Horned Serpent, the a serpent, usually aquatic, common
in various Native American mythologies; may have
crystalline scales prized for their divining powers

hornwork cuckoldry; [archaic]

horripilate having one's hair stand on end; experiencing goose bumps or piloerection; to bristle in horror; [noun: *horripilation*]

horrisonant or **horrisonous** sounding dreadful; uttering a terrible sound

horror vacui (hoar-er vack-yew-eye) the dislike of empty spaces; the aversion to empty space in artistic painting; [Latin *fear of empty space*]

hot tower a tropical cumulonimbus cloud stretching from the troposphere to the stratosphere, which sometimes contributes to cyclones

houri a nymph in the form of a beautiful virgin supposed to dwell in paradise; any voluptuous, beautiful woman; [Persian]

hoverslam or **suicide burn** landing a rocket using thrust

howlround loud squealing sound caused when a microphone is too close to speakers

Human Drift, The an 1894 book detailing a Utopian social plan that centered around a porcelain metropolis of 90 million people at Niagara Falls – a single, publicly-owned company would replace all competitive corporations

Humpty Doo a town in Australia's Northern Territory

Hydra of Lerna or **the Hydra** in Greek and Roman myth., a dragon-like creature with many heads that regenerated when cut off – its breath was poisonous and the mere scent of its blood deadly; [adj. *Hydra-headed*]

Hyperion one of the twelve Titans; father of Helios (sun), Selene (moon), and Eos (Dawn); also a moon of Saturn; [Greek myth.]

hypertridimensional having more than three dimensions

hypnagogic or **hypnogogic** of or relating to the state of consciousness just before sleep; sleep-inducing; applied to the illusions of one who is half asleep; [from *Hypnos*, the god of sleep in Greek myth.];

"*Finnegans Wake* is a kind of *hypnagogic* structure, words reverberating on themselves without pointing to objects...This may be the hallucinatory verbal world within which God speaks."
– Northrop Frye, Canadian literary critic

hypnogenic producing sleep or hypnosis

hypnopompic referring to the state of consciousness before fully awakening; [Greek *hypnos* (sleep) + *pompe* (sending away)]

Hypnos the god of sleep; his twin brother is Thanatos, the god of death; [Greek myth.];
"So gently upon the threshold you plunder
(slipping through what purple-hilled wonder)
yet now dare tease *Hypnos* awake?"
– Robin Devoe, *Dare Tease Hypnos*

I

Iceberg Capital of the World, The a nickname for Twillingate, Newfoundland & Labrador, Canada

icedrake a dragon that breathes ice or has a low body temperature; [fantasy]

ichor an ethereal fluid flowing through the veins of the gods in place of blood; [Greek myth.]

ignescent emitting sparks of fire when struck with steel; having a volatile mood; [Latin *ignis* fire]

ignicolist someone who worships fire

ignipotent having power over fire; fiery; [poetic]

ignis fatuus a phosphorescent light that appears by night over marshy ground and comes from gases released by organic decay; also called *friar's lantern* or *will-o'-the-wisp*; a misleading influence; a decoy; [Latin *foolish fire*]

ignivomous vomiting fire, as an *ignivomous* volcano

Iguanadon a genus of large, herbivorous dinosaur; [*iguana*-tooth]

Ilium poetic name for Troy, the city under seige in Homer's *Iliad*; [Latin]

illachrymable not capable of crying

illth poverty; the opposite of wealth; something the owning of which causes damage

Illyria ancient region in the west Balkans inhabited by tribes collectively known as Illyrians

imago an idealized mental image; the final stage of an insect's metamorphosis

imbricate to place overlapping one another;
"...generations of daedal forest
imbricate distant-dreaming slopes..."
– Robin Devoe, *Dynasties of Artistic Woodland*

imbriferous rainy; pertaining to rain; causing rain;
[Latin *imbrifer* rain-bearing]

imbrute to degrade to the state of a brute; to make brutal;
"The soul grows clotted by contagion, imbodies, and
imbrutes, till she quite lose /
The divine property of her first being." – John Milton
"We are all sculptors and painters, and our material is
our own flesh and blood and bones. Any nobleness
begins at once to refine a man's features, any meanness
or sensuality to *imbrute* them." – Henry David Thoreau

immarcescible unfading; imperishable; lasting;
"I did not think to see them once again,
For what could bring into an old woman's dream
Canova's *immarcescible* marble lovers?"
– Kathleen Raine, 20th c. British poet

impalace to place in a palace

imparadise to put in a state like paradise; to make
supremely happy; to enrapture; to make somewhere
into a paradise; "*imparadised* in one another's arms"
– Milton, *Paradise Lost*

imparity inequality; unable to be equally divided

imperatrix an empress; [archaic]

imperium an empire; absolute power; [Latin]

implex intricate; entangled; complicated; complex

implumous having neither plumes nor feathers

imponderabilia things that are difficult to comprehend; things that are imponderable

impuberal not mature; not having reached puberty

impudent purposely disrespectful; insolent; impertinent; [noun: *impudence*]

inamorata (masculine: *inamorato*) a woman in love; a mistress; [Italian]

inaurate gilded; gleaming; appearing gold-covered

increscent increasing in brightness; waxing, as in the Moon; [adj.]

incurious not curious or inquisitive; without care for or interest in; inattentive

Indra's net an infinitely large net hanging over the Vedic deity Indra's palace on the sacred five-peaked Mount Meru — each vertex of the net holds a multifaceted jewel, which is reflected in all the other jewels; [Hinduism]

infaust not favorable; unlucky; unpropitious; sinister; [archaic]; "While we, alas! must still obambulate, Sequacious of the court and courtier's fate; O most *infaust* who optates there to live! An aulic life no solid joys can give."
 – François Rabelais, 16th c. French Renaissance monk

infinite monkey theorem theorem stating that a monkey typing at random would eventually produce a text (such as Shakespeare's *Hamlet*) given an infinite amount of time; the probability, however, even of monkeys filling the entire observable universe reproducing a complete work such as *Hamlet* within a time period of 100,000 times the universe's age is extremely low

inflatus inspiration; a blowing or breathing into; "The divine breath that blows the nostrils out to ineffable *inflatus*."
 – Elizabeth Barrett Browning, 19th c. English poet

infracaninophile someone who loves, supports, or appreciates underdogs; [coined by 20th c. American writer Christopher Morley]

inglenook a nook or corner near an open fireplace

inglorious not glorious; not bringing honor or glory;
  shameful; disgraceful; ignominious;
  "Death is nothing, but to live defeated and *inglorious*
  is to die daily." – Napoleon

ingluvious gluttonous; [obsolete]

ingravidate to impregnate; [obsolete]

inkhorn term an obscure, overly pretentious borrowing
  from another language; [*inkhorns* are small ink
  containers made of horn]

innubilous cloudless; [obsolete]

inquiline an animal that lives in the nest of another animal

inquorate not having a quorum, or the minimum number
  of members necessary to officially conduct a meeting's
  business and to vote

inscape the unique inner nature or essence of a person
  or thing, esp. as expressed in poetry or other arts;
  the landscape of an indoor area

inselberg or **monadnock** an isolated rock hill, knob, ridge,
  or small mountain rising abruptly from a surrounding
  plain; [German *Insel* (island) + *Berg* (mountain)]

insinuendo an insinuation that includes innuendo

insusurration the act of speaking softly into something

intempestive out of season; untimely; inopportune

interamnian situated between rivers

interaulic existing between royal courts, as an *interaulic* feud

interbellic relating to a time period between wars (an
  interbellum), esp. to the period between WWI and WWII

intercolline situated between hills, esp. applied to valleys
  lying between volcanic cones; [geology]

interfluve in geology, the area of higher land between two
  connected river valleys

intergrade to change from one state to another in
  stages, as pupa to butterfly; an intermediate stage;
  [verb & noun]

interjacent lying or being between or among; [adj.]

interlacustrine situated between lakes, esp. the large lakes around the East African Rift

interlard to mix fat with lean; to interpose; to insert between; to mix or mingle, esp. to introduce that which is foreign or irrelevant; [noun: *interlardment*]

interlucation the act of thinning trees to let in light

interlucent shining between; [poetic; archaic];

"A lurid change is on the face of earth;
And not an *interlucent* star looks forth
To mitigate the gloom."
– Henry Austen Driver, 19th c. British poet

Intermarium a proposed federation of post-WWI countries incl. Finland, Latvia, Lithuania, Estonia, Belarus, Poland, Ukraine, Czechoslovakia, Yugoslavia, Romania & Hungary – an area generally situated between the Baltic, Black, and Adriatic Seas; [Latinized name *between the seas*]

interminable endless; boundless; going on seemingly forever; "Life is before you,– not earthly life alone, but life – a thread running *interminably* through the warp of eternity." – J. G. Holland, American novelist and poet
"So evenings die, in their green going,
A wave, *interminably* flowing." – Wallace Stevens

intermontane between or among mountains

interpluvial a drier geologic period occurring between periods of higher than average precipitation; [noun]

interstellar medium the matter that exists within galaxies but outside solar systems – mostly dust, gas, and cosmic rays

intervale a low-lying, flat piece of land, esp. straddling a river

Iram of the Pillars or **Ubar** a lost city on the Arabian Peninsula mentioned in the Quran and called *Atlantis of the Sands* by Lawrence of Arabia, who wanted to search for it by airship, but never did

ironbound bound as with iron; rugged, as an *ironbound* coast; rigid; unyielding

isabelline or **isabella** a pale grey-yellow or pale cream-brown color; [possibly from the color of *Isabella* of Castile's undergarments – unwashed throughout an eight-month seige of Grenada starting in 1491]

isangelous equal to the angels; [obsolete]

Isle of Seven Cities or **Antilia** a 15th century phantom island thought to lie west of Portugal – from an old Iberian legend of seven Christian Visigothic bishops fleeing Muslim conquerors by sailing west to an island

isoneph line on a map indicating equal cloud cover; [Ancient Greek *ísos* (equal) + *néphos* (cloud)]

ithyphallic pertaining to an erect penis or phallus, esp. in art

izles sparks or embers floating out of a chimney

izzard an old word for the letter Z; [Scotland]

J

jaculus (pl. *jaculi*) in Greek myth., a small winged serpent or dragon, sometimes with front legs; AKA *javeline snake*; "The *jaculus* darts from the branches of trees; ...as though... hurled from an engine." – Pliny; [Latin *thrown*]

janegirl a boy who behaves in a stereotypically girlish manner; a tomgirl; [rare]

jawfallen dejected; [archaic]

jebel or **djebel** hill or mountain; [Arabic]; "Otherways wesways like that provost scoffing bedoueen the *jebel* and the jypsian sea..." – James Joyce, *Finnegans Wake*

jeunesse dorée young people of fashionable society; very rich youth; [French *gilded youth*]

jill may refer to the female of several animals, incl. ferret, rabbit, hare, kangaroo, opossum, wallaby, weasel, and wombat

jiva in Hinduism, the essence of the individual soul

jnana knowledge gained through meditation that identifies one's self with ultimate reality (Hinduism); pure

awareness free of conceptual thinking (Buddhism);
[Sanskrit *jñāna* knowledge]

Jotunheim in Norse myth., home of the giants

joypop to take drugs in a recreational way without
becoming addicted; [slang]

jumboism fondness or admiration for large things;
liking something simply because it is large

juneberry a small North American tree of the genus
Amelanchier, which includes sarvis, saskatoon,
mountain shadbush, and snowy mespilus

K

kairos a favorable time for a decision or action;
an opportune moment; [Greek *kairós* opportunity]

Kalma Finnish death-goddess that smells of decaying flesh;
[related word: Finnish *kalmisto* (graveyard)]

kalon ideal perfect beauty; deeper, more than superficial
beauty; [related: Greek *kállos* beauty]

kalopsia the delusion that things are more beautiful than
they really are; [Ancient Greek *kalós* (good, beautiful) +
ópsis (view)]

kalpa aeon; a long period of time equal to 1000 yumas
or 4.32 billion years; [Sanskrit *kalpa* formation]

Kalpavriksha a divine tree that grants wishes in Hinduism,
Jainism, and Buddhism; [Sanskrit *world tree*]

Karakum or **Gara-Gum Desert** desert covering 70% of
Turkmenistan; [Turkmen *garagum* (black or dark sand)]

karoshi death from working too hard; [Japanese]

Kartlis Deda a monument in Tbilisi of a woman symbolizing
the Georgian national character – she holds a bowl of
wine to greet friends, a sword to greet enemies;
[Georgian *mother of Georgia*]

katzenjammer hangover; anguish; depression; clamor;
uproar; [German, literally: *wailing of cats*]

kelpie a mischievous shape-shifting spirit, often in the form
of a horse, believed to haunt rivers and lochs in Scotland

and warn of, or sometimes assist in, drownings; [Celtic myth.]

kenning a far off view, esp. at sea; as far as one can see (about 20 miles at sea); a wee portion

kenspeckle having so marked an appearance as to be easily recognized; [Scotland]

khamsin a hot, perhaps sand-filled, Saharan wind; esp. such a wind in Egypt, which sometimes blows for about 50 days; [Egyptian Arabic *ḳamsīn* fifty]

kill box mate a box-shaped checkmate pattern in chess utilizing a rook and a queen

kinderspiel a play or musical performed by children; something that is easily done; [German, literally: *children's game*]

kindle collective term for kittens

kirkbuzzer thief who robs churches; [British; archaic]

kirkgarth a churchyard; [Northern England]

kith friends and acquaintances; kindred; [archaic]

kraken large sea monster in Norse myth., usually with tentacles; [Norwegian *kraken* (sea monster)];
"Below the thunders of the upper deep,
Far, far beneath in the abysmal sea,
His ancient, dreamless, uninvaded sleep
The *Kraken* sleepeth..." – Alfred, Lord Tennyson

krummholz trees in subarctic and subalpine treeline areas deformed by exposure to cold winds and tending to grow nearer the ground then they otherwise would; elfinwood; [German *krumm* (crooked, bent, twisted) + *Holz* (wood)]

kulshedra in Albanian myth., a water, storm, and fire demon in the form of a female serpentine dragon with several heads; causes natural disasters and is defeated by a winged divine semi-human wielding a lightning-sword; [Latin *chersydrus* (amphibious snake)]

Kummerspeck excess weight gained from emotional overeating; [German *Kummer* (grief) + *Speck* (bacon)]

kvell to express happiness, joy, or pride, esp. in satisfaction of one or more family members; [Yiddish *kveln*]

L

labellum the lower petal of an orchid, often curiously shaped; [Latin *labellum* (small tub)];
"When *labellum* quiver, and moist lotus quake..."

lachrymal or **lacrimal** relating to tears; [Latin *lacrima* tear]

lachrymist one who cries or weeps, esp. if frequently

lachrymogenic causing weeping; tear-creating

Lacrima Christi an Italian wine produced on the slopes of Mount Vesuvius and mentioned in Dumas's *The Count of Monte Cristo*, Voltaire's *Candide*, and a Christopher Marlow play; according to local myth, Christ's tears (from lamenting Lucifer's fall from heaven) fertilized the soil with divine inspiration; [Italian *tears of Christ*]

Lake Boonderoo an ephemeral lake in SW Australia; [Australian Aboriginal word for *stony country*]

Lake Elphinstone an Australian lake; [Scottish-born explorer George *Elphinstone* Dalrymple]

Lake Stevens Monster the largest known glacial erratic (a boulder) in Washington State

Lamaria a Georgian goddess of the hearth derived from Jesus's mother Mary – esp. honored in the Svaneti region

lamia in Greek myth., a monster (sometimes with a woman's head & breasts and a snake's lower body) capable of fully assuming a woman's form who devours humans or sucks children's blood; a female demon; a vampire; a sorceress;
"Philosophy will clip an Angel's wings,
Conquer all mysteries by rule and line,
Empty the haunted air, and gnomed mine—
Unweave a rainbow, as it erewhile made
The tender-person'd *Lamia* melt into a shade."
– John Keats, 19th c. English Romantic poet

Land of Nod mentioned in *Genesis* as being "east of Eden," the place Cain was exiled to after murdering his brother Abel; [later associated with sleep & dreams from works by Jonathon Swift and Robert Louis Stevenson]

landblink a brightness in the air observed from sea when looking toward far, snow-covered lands in Arctic regions

Land of the Eternal Blue Sky Mongolia; [poetic]; [Mongolian *Munkh Khukh Tengriin Oron*]

Land of the Living Skies nickname for Saskatchewan, Canada

Land of the Long White Cloud poetic name for New Zealand; [Maori *Aotearoa*]

Larissa a moon of Neptune; [from *Larissa*, a nymph and lover of Poseidon in Greek myth.]

larmoyant tearful; tearfully sentimental; [French *larme* tear]

latrinalia deliberate markings or words inscribed on surfaces in public restrooms; bathroom graffiti

Laurasia a supercontinent that separated from Gondwana circa 200 BCE and later broke apart as the North Atlantic Ocean opened; [*Laurentia + Asia*]

laurence a shimmering above a hot surface, such as a road – from irregular refraction of light; [rare]

Leading Tickles a town in Newfoundland & Labrador, Canada

leafy seadragon an Australian marine fish (in the seahorse family) with long leaf-like protrusions

leitmotif or **leitmotiv** in music, a melodic passage or phrase, esp. in Wagnerian opera, associated with a specific character, situation, or element; a dominant and recurring theme, as in a novel

lemniscate the infinity symbol; ∞

Lemuria a continent falsely hypothesized to have sunk beneath the Indian Ocean and to being humankind's ancestral home; [adj. *Lemurian*]

Lepontic an extinct Alpine Celtic language, once spoken in what is now northern Italy

leptogenic describing something that causes weight loss; [Ancient Greek *leptós* thin]

Lethe oblivion; forgetfulness; in Greek myth., one of five rivers in Hades (the underworld), the drinking from which caused total forgetfulness of past life; "No *Lethean* drug for Eastern lands..."
– John Greenleaf Whittier, American Quaker poet
"Thou hast conquered, O pale Galilean;
The world has grown gray from thy breath;
We have drunken from things *Lethean*,
And fed on the fullness of death."
– Algernon Charles Swinburne, English poet

lethiferous deadly; bringing death or destruction

levanter an easterly wind that blows from the Mediterranean Sea toward the Atlantic Ocean

leviathan a dangerous & powerful biblical sea serpent; something very large or incredibly dominating in wealth, influence, etc.; a domineering government; "Summation of *Leviathan*: 'The axiom, fear; the method, logic; the conclusion, despotism.'" – Hugh Trevor-Roper, 20th c. English historian

lexiconophilist one who loves and/or collects word books or dictionaries

lexis all words (or a unified subset of words) in a given language; the vocabulary used by a particular writer

Libertalia a pirate colony founded in Madagascar in the late 17th century by a French captain – likely only legendary; [Latin *liber* free]

Libyan Desert glass or **Great Sand Sea glass** a type of glass – possibly of meteoritic origin

lickdish or **lick-box** a glutton; a lover of fine food; [obsolete]

lickerish eager; greedy to swallow; eager to taste or enjoy; lecherous; lusty

lickpenny a devourer or absorber of money; a miser; "Law is a *lickpenny*" – Sir Walter Scott

lickport an opening thru which a caged animal can lick water or other drink

lightwell an opening providing light from above; [architecture]

lilac-breasted roller a colorful bird widely distributed in sub-Saharan Africa – an acrobatic flier and the national bird of Kenya

Lilliputian a very small person or thing; of a very small size; diminutive; [from *Lilliput*, an imaginary island in *Gulliver's Travels* by Anglo-Irish satirist Jonathan Swift]

limerance or **limerence** the initial rush of romantic love; the state of being in love; an involuntary state of intense desire; [adj. *limerent*]; [coined by American psychologist Dorothy Tennov in 1979]

Lion Has Wings, The a prominent and historically persuasive British propoganda war film highlighting the Royal Air Force – released in 1939, near the start of WWII

litterfall organic parts of plants that fall off, most commonly leaves from trees; leaf litter

logan a rocking or nearly balanced stone

Lonesome Sundown nickname for American blues musician Cornelius Green III (1928-1995)

long drop outhouse; [New Zealand slang]

long pig human meat as human food

lookoff a scenic viewpoint

lords and ladies a common name for *arum maculatum*, a woodland flowering plant found in Europe, Turkey, and the Caucasus

Loris a genus of slow-moving, nocturnal, arboreal primates native to India & Sri Lanka

lorn lonely, abandoned; lost; ruined; forlorn; [archaic]
"Yet, trust me, Memory's warmest sighs
Are often breathed in moments *lorn* –
And many a feeling thought will rise
And in the bosom die unborn."
– Gerald Griffin, 19th c. Irish poet

Lost Monarch a coast redwood tree in Northern California discovered in 1998 and 98 meters tall – the world's 5th largest coast redwood by volume

lotophagous lotus-eating; lazy; day-dreamy

lotus eater a person who indulges in pleasure, luxury, or easeful living rather than attending to practical matters; [from island dwellers who fed on the fruit of the *lotus* tree in Homer's *Odyssey*]

Lovecraftian terrifying in a monstrous or alien way; akin to the writing style of H. P. Lovecraft

love-in-a-mist a common name of *nigella damascena*, a flowering plant native to southern Europe, north Africa, and southwest Asia

lovestone ivy plant; [British]; [From the manner in which ivy covers and clings to stone walls]

lucida the brightest star in a given constellation; any easily visible star

lucific producing light; [Latin *lūx* (light) + *facere* (to make)]

lucifugous shunning, avoiding, or disliking light; nocturnal

lucriferous profitable; [obsolete]

ludibund playful; sportive; [Latin *ludibundus*]; [archaic]

ludic playful in a spontaneous or aimless manner; relating to play or playfulness

luftmensch (pl. *luftmenschen*) an impractical dreamer, esp. one without regular income; one more concerned with fanciful intellectual pursuits than with practical matters; [Yiddish *luftmentsh* airman]

lumen (pl. *lumina*) derived unit of luminous flux – the total quantity of visible light emitted over time

luminiferous aether in obsolete, late 19th century physics, the postulated medium for the propagation of light

lumpenproletariat the lowest, most degraded subclass of the working class (the proletariat); [German *Lumpen* rag]

lustral of, pertaining to, or used for purification, as *lustral* days or *lustral* water; purifying

Lyran adjectival form of Lyra, a small constellation that includes the bright star Vega; "Proposals on interstellar trade dominated the *Lyran* ambassador's diplomacy."

lyrical dissonance when the emotions evoked by a song's lyrics don't match the music

M

MacGillycuddy's Reeks an Irish mountain range

mackerel sky cirrocumulus or altocumulus clouds set in rows and displaying a pattern similar to fish scales – often heralds wet weather

macushla my darling; [Irish *mo chuisle* (my pulse)]

madstone a stone fancied to heal the bite of a poisonous animal; [American folklore]

maenad a female in Bacchanal or Dionysian rites; a frenzied or very wild woman; [adj. *maenadic*]

maggotorium a place where maggots are grown or stored, usually for fishing

Mag Mell an island paradise of eternal happiness and beauty west of Ireland (or a realm beneath the sea) reached thru death or glory; [Irish myth.]

magnetosphere the region of space surrounding an astronomical body in which its magnetic field predominates

Mahdist War an 1881-1899 war between the Mahdist Sudanese and the Khedivate of Egypt & Britain; [the Sudanese leader proclaimed himself the *Mahdi* (guided one) of Islam]

maliferous unhealthy; dangerous; [archaic]

mallemaroking the carousing aboard icebound Greenland whaling ships; [likely Dutch-derived]

Malvern Hills hills known for their spring water near the western English spa town of Great Malvern; [Welsh *moelfryn* (bald hill)]

Mama Killa or **Mama Quilla** in Incan myth., a moon goddess of great beauty that protected women and cried tears of silver – lunar eclipses were caused by her being attacked by an animal; [Quechua language *mama* (mother) + *killa* (moon)]

mamelon a small round hill; [French *mamelon* nipple]

mammatus or **mammatocumulus** a type of cloud with breast-shaped pouches extending below – may portend violent storms when attached to cumulonimbus

mammonism debased devotion to the pursuit of wealth; [Latin *mammona* wealth; Aramaic *māmōnā* money]

mansuetude gentleness; meekness; mildness; tameness; [archaic]

mantic of, like, or pertaining to divination; prophetic; inspired by a divine source

manticore beast with a lion body, a scorpion tail, and a human head with rows of sharp teeth and the ability to shoot spikes from its tail to paralyze prey – may be horned or winged, with a voice the mixture of pipes and trumpets; [Persian and Greek myth.]

mantric of or related to a mantra, a word or phrase repeated to aid concentration during meditation; of or related to a mystical incantation

marcescent withered, but still attached – as in a blossom; "How often is the flower of human life *marcescent*, tenacious of its old estate when the blooming-time is past." – Edith M. Thomas, American poet

mardy moody or grumpy; miserable; sulky; [England]

Mare Imbrium a large, lunar crater formed during the Late Heavy Bombardment; [Latin *Sea of Showers*]

maremma a marshy seaside area, esp. in Italy

marigenous produced in or by the sea

Marilyn one of 2011 mountains or hills in the British Isles with a prominence higher than 150 meters (492 feet); [punning coinage riffing off *Marilyn* Monroe and homophonous *munro* (Scottish mountain over 3000 ft)]

marivaudage in the style of 18th c. French writer Marivaux; an affectation of refinement in writing

Marlovian akin or relating to 16th c. English writer Christopher Marlowe – he popularized blank verse, was probably a government spy, and may have authored some or all of Shakespeare's works

marmalise or **marmalize** to thrash; to beat up; to defeat soundly, as in a sporting event; [British; possibly from *marmalade + pulverize*]

marmoreal like marble; cold or aloof, like a marble statue; "For in no wise could he leave that lofty spot, or descend the wide *marmoreal* flights." – Howard Phillips Lovecraft

marquess or **marquis** (feminine: *marchioness*) British title of nobility ranked above earl & beneath duke

maunder wander without aim; mutter; speak indistinctly; talk rapidly, vapidly, and incessantly

mazarine a deep, rich blue color

meadowhawk type of North American dragonfly of the genus *Sympetrum*

meatsuit a physical body, when temporarily worn (inhabited) by a demon or spirit; [fantasy]

medusahead a bristly grass plant native to Europe

meeping making a high-pitched exclamation

megaprime prime number of at least a million digits

mellifluent or **mellifluous** smooth-flowing; musical and sweet-sounding; flowing like honey; [noun: *mellifluence*]; "*Mellifluous* Shakespeare, whose enchanting Quill Commandeth Mirth or Passion, was but Will." – Thomas Heywood, 17th c. English playwright

melliloquent sweet and harmonious in speech; [Latin *mellis* (honey) + *loquens* (speaking)]

mellisonant sweet-sounding

mellisugent honey-sucking, esp. as a bird or insect

Melusina a freshwater spirit in the form of a woman with a serpent or fish-like lower body, and sometimes wings or two tails; [Celtic myth.]

memory span the maximum number of different items, such as numbers, that an average person can memorize with relative ease

menacme (MEN-ack-mee) the time of life when a human female is menstruating, between *menarche* & *menopause*

mephitine of, pertaining to, or like a skunk

mephitis a foul exhalation from decomposing substances or other sources; a stench; an unpleasantly odorous or poisonous gas, esp. emitted from the earth; [adj. *mephitic*]

merrythought a bird's furcula, or wishbone; [from the hopeful thoughts often attending its ritual breakage]

meshuga crazy; stupid or foolish; [Yiddish *meshuge*]

metal umlaut or **röck döts** a diacritical mark often used decoratively in the names of metal, punk, or hard rock bands such as the American bands Blue Öyster Cult, Hüsker Dü, and Mötley Crüe

metaphrase a word-for-word translation from one language to another; an answering phrase, as in repartee

metaverse a conceptual whole universe made up of some or all other universes; a future internet where users can interact in a virtual-reality space; [*meta* + *universe*]

metempirical beyond or outside of direct experience; transcendental

methanogenetic pertaining to the generation of methane by anaerobic bacteria

mickey the smallest distance you can move a computer mouse – roughly 1/500 of an inch; [from the cartoon character *Mickey* Mouse]

microcentury one millionth of a century – about 52 minutes and 36 seconds; "Professor Dotard's lecture lasted literally two *microcenturies!*"

microfortnight one millionth of a fortnight – 1.2 seconds

microhenry one millionth of a henry, a unit of electrical inductance; [Joseph *Henry*, 19th c. American scientist]

microlambert one millionth of a lambert – a unit of luminance; [Johann *Lambert*, 18th c. Swiss physicist];

"So disappointed that any brightness in her eyes was best measured in *microlamberts.*"

micromort a unit of risk equal to a one-in-a-million chance of dying

microprobability a one-in-a-million chance that a certain event will happen

middenstead a place where dung is piled

milliard a billion; [rare]

milliHelen amount of beauty needed to launch just one ship; [based on a reference to *Helen* of Troy in Marlowe's play *Doctor Faustus*: "Was this the face that launch'd a thousand ships, And burnt the topless towers of Ilium..."]

Miltonic relating or akin to the works or style of 17th c. English poet John Milton; "Her garden at dawn seems a *Miltonic* Eden of golden dreams."

minced oath a euphemistic expression formed by replacing an objectionable word (usually near the original in spelling or pronunciation) with a substitute that renders the phrase more socially acceptable; "*Gosh freaking darnit*, I wish he'd *shut the front door!*"

mindsight awareness of one's own patterns of thinking in order to correct undesirable behaviors or thoughts

mindstyle an habitual manner of thinking

minibeast a small creature, esp. an insect or spider; [British]

minimoon a short honeymoon or romantic vacation

mirabilia wonders; marvels; [Latin]

mirkning late twilight; dusk; [Scottish]

mirrorwork bits of reflective metal attached to clothing

mirrorscope an old-fashioned slide projector

mise en abyme self-reflection or introspection in a literary or other artistic work; the representation of the whole work embedded in a work; [French, literally: *placement into abyss*]

misly or **mizzly** (adj.) rain with very small drops; misty; [noun & verb: *mizzle*]

mistpouffer a mysterious or unexplained sound heard over the ocean, esp. a booming sound in foggy weather off the coast of Belgium or the Netherlands

Mithrim Montes the highest mountain range on Saturn's moon Titan; [all mountains on Titan are named after mountains in J.R.R. Tolkien's writings]

mizmaze a maze or labyrinth; bewilderment; [obsolete]

modena deep purple; a shade of crimson; [from *Modena*, an Italian city and province]

mollipilose downy; soft; having soft hairs or plumage; [Latin *mollis* (soft) + *pilosus* (hairy)]

Mongolian death worm a nearly meter-long worm supposedly living deep in the Gobi Desert and killing by spraying venom or by electrocution

Monkey's Eyebrow a town in western Kentucky; [originally two towns: Old Monkey & New Monkey]

Monoceros a faint, equatorial constellation just east of Orion; [Greek *unicorn*]

monochrome rainbow or **red rainbow** a rare type of rainbow that may occur when the sun is near the horizon

montagnard a person who lives in the mountains; mountain-dwelling; [noun and adj.]; [French]

Montes Rook a circular mountain range on the Moon; [from English astronomer Lawrence *Rooke*]

montigenous produced on a mountain; from the mountains

moonblink temporary blindness or sight impairment once thought to be caused by sleeping in the moonlight

moonglade or **moonwake** the bright reflection of the Moon's light on an expanse of water; [poetic]

moon-splashed covered by patches of moonlight

moontime the time when human females are menstruating

morceau (pl. *morceaux*) a morsel; a small piece; a short passage of literature or musical composition; [French]

More Tomorrow a village in Belize

Morpheus the winged god of dreams; one of the thousand sons of Somnus (god of sleep) – collectively termed the Somnia (dream shapes); [likely from Ovid's *Metamorphoses*]

mortlake an oxbow lake; [British]

mother-out-law the mother of an ex-wife or ex-husband – in contradistinction to *mother-in-law*; [US slang]

Mountains of Kong a legendary mountain range charted on African maps during the 1800's – thought to stretch from Guinea in West Africa east to the Mountains of the Moon (also legendary); [*Kong*, a town in northern Ivory Coast and former capital of the Kong Empire]

Mountains of the Moon legendary mountain range in East Africa once thought to be the source of the Nile; [supposedly named for being snowcapped and therefore white like the Moon]

Mount Damavand 5609-meter Persian peak, the highest in the Middle East and highest volcano (possibly active) in Asia – a symbol of resistance against illegitimate rule in Persian poetry

Mount Kailash a Tibetan mountain sacred to Hinduism, Buddhism, Jainism, and Bon (a pre-Buddhist religion of Tibet); [perhaps from Sanskrit *kelāsa* (crystal)]

Mount Shimbiris the highest peak in Somaliland in the Horn of Africa at 2460 meters

moxie bravery; determination; energy; skill

Mu a legendary lost continent, sometimes associated with Atlantis or Lemuria

muciferous conveying or secreting mucus

mucopurulent having the character or appearance of both mucus and pus

muculent slimy; moist and viscous; like mucus

multiversant turning into many shapes; assuming many forms

mundivagant wandering around the world

murderbird a shrike – a bird that impales its victims

murmurous (adj.) describing a low and indistinct sound, like murmuring; "And if she speaks in her frail way, / it is wholly to bewitch / my smallest thought with a most swift / radiance wherein slowly drift / *murmurous* things divinely bright." – E. E. Cummings, 20th c. American poet

murrey a dark red or mulberry color

musard a dreamer; an absent-minded person; [obsolete]

music of the spheres an ancient philosophical concept that the orbital movement of celestial bodies, such as planets, produce a type of music

Muspelheim or **Muspell** one of the nine worlds in Norse myth., full of fire, light, and heat; home to the fire giants and guarded by the flaming sword of Surtr; *Muspelheim* is also a star, invisible to the naked eye, over 1000 light years from Earth

mystagogic pertaining to the teaching of, or initiation into, mysteries; [noun: *mystagogue*]

mysterianism a philosophical stance that the mystery of consciousness will never be understood by humans

mysterium tremendum a very big or overwhelming mystery, esp. the mystery of God; [Latin *awe-inspiring mystery*]

mystery snail a river snail native to South America

mythologem a basic and universal mythic theme such as honor, self-sacrifice, or a universal flood

mythopoetic giving rise to myths; pertaining to the creation of myth; [noun: *mythopoet*]

myxoid pertaining to or resembling mucus; [Ancient Greek *muxa* slime]

N

Naglfar in Norse myth., a boat fashioned entirely from fingernails and toenails of the dead; [Old Norse *nail farer*]

naiad a water nymph (type of female deity) supposed to preside over a body of fresh water, such as a spring, lake,

or stream; [Greek myth.]
"Hast thou not torn the *Naiad* from her flood,
The Elfin from the green grass, and from me
The summer dream beneath the tamarind tree?"
– Edgar Allan Poe, *Sonnet – To Science*

nanobreak a microvacation; a very brief vacation or respite from everyday life

nanofluidics the study of fluids confined to nanometer scale structures

narcosis or **narcoma** drug-induced unconsciousness

natal cleft or **intergluteal cleft** the groove bisecting human buttocks

Natalia Republic a Boer republic (1839-1843) founded after a Voortrekker victory over Zulus in the Battle of Blood River; [the area was discovered by Portuguese sailors on *Natal* (Christmas)]

near-miss Johnson solid in geometry, a complex polyhedron with imprecisely regular faces

nebris the fawn-skin worn by Dionysus (god of wine, madness, ecstasy) and his followers; [Greek myth.]

necrogenic causing necrosis; originating from dead organic material; [adj.]

necrosis localized death of bodily cells or tissues; death of plant cells; [adj. *necrotic*]; "The fragrant decay of Autumn's sweet *necrosis* filled the wood, recalling his fondest boyhood days."

necroscopy or **necropsy** the medical examination of a dead body, esp. to find the cause of death; [adj. *necroscopic*]

nefandous unspeakable; extremely vile or wicked

nemophilist one who is fond of forests; a haunter of the woods; [adj. *nemophilous*]

nemorous woodsy; shady and treed

neophobic describing that which fears or dislikes new things or experiences; such a person or animal; [adj. & noun]

Neotropical realm one of Earth's eight ecozones (biogeographic realms) – mostly covering Central and South America

nepenthe (ni-PEN-thee) something, esp. a drink, that causes one to forget their troubles or their suffering; [adj. *nepenthean*]; [from a drug mentioned in Homer's *Odyssey* as a grief remedy]

nepheliad a cloud nymph

nepheligenous discharging clouds of smoke, esp. of tobacco; [Ancient Greek *nephélē* cloud]

nephelosphere cloudy envelope surrounding a planet

Nephilim a race of heroic giants (or fallen angels) mentioned early in the Bible; [Hebrew *nefilim* (fallen ones)]

nephogram a photograph of clouds

ne plus ultra the highest achievement; perfection; the ultimate; the most perfect example; [Latin *not more beyond*]

neritic of or pertaining to ocean waters near the coast and overlying a continental shelf

nestcock a househusband; a delicate man who stays at home; "Often home, but certainly no *nestcock*: his ventures afield both vigorous and brave."

neverwet flowering plant with waxy leaves that repel water

Niflheim one of the nine worlds consisting of misty, cold lands and nine frozen rivers; the realm of Hel, goddess of the dead; [Norse myth.]

nightgear nightclothes; garments worn in bed

nightpiece a painting or literary passage depicting or describing a night scene

Nine Barrow Down an elongated English hill with nine barrows (stone age burial mounds) upon it

Nine Mothers of Heimdallr the nine sisters who bore the god Heimdallr, who watches for invaders from where the rainbow bridge Bifrost meets the sky; [Norse myth.]

niveous snowy; resembling snow;
 "Cottage, and steeple, in the *niveous* stole / Of Winter
 trimly dressed." – James Hurdis, 18th c. English poet
noblebright a subgenre of fantasy fiction wherein the hero
 completes a quest and good triumphs over evil;
 [opposite of subgenre *grimdark*]
noctiferous bringing night; [obsolete]
noctilucent glowing in the dark or at night, as in *noctilucent*
 clouds
noctivagant roving or wandering at night
noetic of or pertaining to the mind or thought; originating
 in or understood by reason
nom de guerre (nom-de-gair) a fake name someone uses
 during war or during a competitive, social activity;
 pseudonym; [French, literally: *war name*]
nom de voyage a name assumed during a period of travel;
 traveling name; [French]
noumenon (pl. *noumena*) a thing in itself; a thing which can
 be assumed to exist by reason or intuition as opposed to
 phenomena that are apprehended by the senses;
 [adj. *noumenal*]
novilunar of or pertaining to the new moon
nubiferous bringing, or producing, clouds
nubigenous born of, or produced from, clouds
nubilous cloudy, misty, or foggy; overcast; not clear
nubivagant wandering in the clouds; moving thru the air;
 [Latin *nubes* (cloud) + *vagant* (wandering)]
nulliverse the world viewed as being devoid of any
 rationality, unifying principle, or masterplan;
 "Now, why should an author not create a "*nulliverse*" to
 represent "oneirologically" the contents of his own
 mind?" – John Updike, 20th c. American novelist & poet
numbles edible animal entrails; [Middle French *nombles*
 (loin of meat)]
numen (pl. *numina*) a divinity, esp. a local or presiding god;
 creative energy; something mystical & transcendent

Numidia kingdom in northwest Africa that ended in 40 BCE – a major early state in Berber history

numinous relating to a numen; indicating the presence of a divinity; awe-inspiring; evoking a sense of the transcendent, mystical, or sublime; supernatural, mysterious; spiritual; appealing to lofty emotions or to aesthetic sense; "*Numinous* feelings are the original god-stuff from which the theory-making mind extracts the individualised gods of the pantheon." – Aldous Huxley
"So sweet, this mourning-cloak of loneness cast
upon those thoughts that dared to sing –
yet, melancholic the wake of this that passed
wrapped in feelings of *numinous* dream."
– Robin Devoe, *Bound by Ancient Longing*

nyctophile (nik-toe-file) a lover of night or darkness; [Greek *night-loving*]; [adj. *nyctophilic*]

Nylonkong contraction of **N**ew **Y**ork, **Lon**don, and Hong **Kong**, all global cultural & financial centers – arguably the most remarkable modern cities

O

Oak at the Gate of the Dead a 1000 year old Welsh oak tree near the 1165 Battle of Crogen; [named due to supposed burial site nearby]

obambulate to walk about; to wander without purpose

obdormition the feeling of numbness when a limb "falls asleep"

Oberon king of the fairies in medieval and Renaissance literature; a moon of Uranus

obesogenic causing obesity; [adj.]

oblivescence the action of forgetting; the process of losing the memory of a person, thing, or experience; the state of being forgotten; [noun]

obmutescent speechless; habitually silent; preferring silence or unable to speak; [adj.]

obnubilate overclouded; darkened as by a cloud; to becloud; to obscure; [Latin *ob* (in the way) + *nubilus* (cloudy)]; [adj. & verb]

obtenebrate to darken or make dark; to enshadow a thing; [noun: *obtenebration*]

octothorpe the # symbol, as on telephone pads and keyboards; hash, pound sign, or number sign

oculus in architecture, a circular window or opening; an opening atop a dome; [Latin *eye*]

Odin ruler of the Aesir; father of Thor; associated with knowledge, poetry, and war; rides the eight-legged horse Sleipnir – also the god of magic and inspiration; [Norse myth.]

odorivector any substance that gives off an odor

ogreish or **ogrish** ogre-like in appearance; characteristic of an ogre

oeillade a glance or wink, esp. an amorous one

okta in meteorology, one eighth of the area of the sky (the celestial dome); used as a measure of cloudiness (six oktas means that 3/4 of the sky is obscured, for example)

oleander a poisonous, ornamental shrub with white or rose-colored flowers

olisbos (pl. *olisboi*) an ancient Greek leather phallus stuffed with wool and sometimes used for self-pleasure

olivaster olive-colored

ombrophobia fear of rain; [rare]; [Ancient Greek *ómbros* (rainstorm, deluge)]

Omicron Draconis a giant star in the constellation Draco; the north pole star of Mercury

omniarch world-ruler

omnific or **omnificent** capable of creating or doing anything; all-creating

omniparous producing all things

omnishambles several shambles (big messes) grouped together by time, place, or cause; a very poorly managed situation; [adj. *omnishambolic*]; [British]

omnispective all-seeing

omnitude the condition of being everything; universality

omnivagant wandering everywhere

oneiric dreamy; of or relating to dreams; [Ancient Greek *óneiros* dream]

oneirocritic one who interprets dreams; [adj. *oneirocritical*]

oneiromancy art of predicting the future by interpreting dreams; [adj. *oneiromantic*; noun: *oneiromancer*]

oofy wealthy, rich; "This Tom has a peculiarity I've noticed in other very *oofy* men. Nick him for the paltriest sum, and he lets out a squawk you can hear at Land's End. He has the stuff in gobs, but he hates giving it up."
– P. G. Wodehouse, 20th c. English humorist author

Operation Acid Gambit a 1989 United States Delta Force operation to retrieve a captive American from Panama

Operation Pig Bristle during the Chinese Civil War, a 1946 operation by the Royal Australian Air Force to transport pig bristles from China to Hong Kong and on to Australia to satisfy an acute paintbrush shortage

Ophelian in an unstable, frenzied state; suicidally insane; like or pertaining to Hamlet's sister Ophelia

opsimath one who begins (or continues) a marked path of learning (or study) late in life

orexigenic an appetite stimulant; [Ancient Greek *oréxis* appetite]

orgulous proud; haughty; [Old French *orgoillus* proud]

orichalcum a metal mentioned by Plato in association with Atlantis as second in value only to gold – possibly platinum, bronze, brass or some unknown alloy; [derived from Greek *oros* (mountain) + *chalkos* (copper)]

orison a prayer; deep mystical thought or communion; "And, as Echo far off through the vale my sad *orison* rolls / I think, oh, my love! 'tis thy voice from the Kingdom of Souls..." – Thomas Moore, 19th c. Irish poet

orographic of or pertaining to the physical features or the scientific study of mountains

orpharion a Renaissance stringed musical instrument, similar to the lute; [*Orpheus* (legendary Greek poet & musician) + *Arion* (ancient Greek Dionysiac poet mythically kidnapped by pirates and rescued by dolphins)]

Orphic like Orpheus, the ancient Greek poet and musician; mystic or occult; entrancing

Orphic Egg cosmic egg from which golden-winged Phanes, a primordial deity, hatched entwined with a serpent; Phanes was the seed of gods and men; [Greek myth.]

ortolan bunting a passerine bird native to Europe and western Asia – diners traditionally cover their own heads with napkins while eating this French delicacy; [Middle French *hortolan* gardener]

ostrobogulous (aw-STRUH-bog-yew-lus) slightly indecent; strange, bizarre, or unusual

osculate to kiss; [Latin *ōs* (mouth) + *-culis* (little)]

Osiris Egyptian god of the underworld – green-skinned and mummy-wrapped at the legs; [adj. *Osirian* & *Osiric*]

otherkin or **otherkind** a subculture of people who self-identify (socially and spiritually) as something other than entirely human, such as angels, fairies, sprites, aliens, elves, or dragons

ouroboros (pl. *ouroboroi*) a serpent or dragon who eats its own tail representing totality, completion, or the cycle of life & death; a picture or symbol depicting this; [Ancient Greek *ourobóros* (tail-devouring)]

outfangthief the right of a lord to pursue a thieving vassal outside of his jurisdiction; [as opposed to: *infangthief*]

outmantle to excel in mantling; to excel in splendor, dress, or ornament; "She *outmantles* the setting sun..."

outré or **outre** unconventional or bizarre; beyond what is considered normal; [French]

outremer area beyond the sea; overseas; a brilliant, pure dark blue or slightly purplish color; ultramarine; [French *outre-mer* (beyond the sea)]

overmorrow the day after tomorrow; [archaic]

owllight glimmering or low level light

Oxbridge a collective reference to the UK's two oldest and most prestigious universities: Oxford & Cambridge; may include elitist undertones; [adj. *Oxbridgian*]

polyphiloprogenitive very productive or prolific; [coined in 1919 by British poet T. S. Eliot]

oxland an obsolete unit of land measurement – about 8 acres

oxter armpit; axilla; "...undeodorized *oxters.*" – Anthony Burgess, 20th c. British author

Ozymandian related or akin to Ozymandias, the imagined proud king of Shelley's poem by the same name, whose great empire faded to nothingness

P

Palentine Hill the centermost of Rome's seven hills; in Roman myth. this hill contained the Lupercal, the cave where Romulus and Remus were found and subsequently nourished by the she-wolf Lupa

palpebrate having eyelids; to blink or wink; [adj. & verb]; [Latin *palpebra* eyelid]

palpus (pl. *palpi*) invertebrate appendage

palustrine relating to, or living within, marshes or swamps; marshy; paludal; paludine

Pando AKA *the trembling giant*, a colony of quaking aspen in Utah – the world's heaviest single living organism and one of its oldest; [Latin *I spread*]

panharmonic in universal accord; [Ancient Greek *pân* all]

panivorous eating bread; subsisting on bread; [Latin *panis* bread]

panoptic seeing everything or all things at once; including everything visible in one view

pansophy universal wisdom or knowledge

pantomorphic capable of assuming any form or shape

pantoscopic literally, seeing everything; applied to bifocal eyeglasses and to wide-angle photography

papilla (anatomy) a small, nipple-like projection, such as the *papillae* of the human tongue; [Latin *papilla* nipple]

papoose bag for carrying a small child on your back

paracosm an imaginary world thought out in great detail, esp. one imagined by a child or young person; [Greek *para* (beside) + *kosmos* (world)]

paradiddle sound of a rapidly beaten drum

Paradiski a ski resort in the Tarentaise Valley, France – the valley is arguably home to the world's greatest concentration of world-class ski resorts

paragnosis knowledge gained by supernatural, rather than scientific, means

paralarva a new-born squid, octopus, or other cephalopod

paralian someone who lives by the ocean or sea

paranymph a bridesmaid or bridesman; one who leads the bride to her marriage; a bestman; one who countenances and supports another; an ally

paraph a flourish made with the pen at the end of a signature (employed as a safeguard against forgery in the Middle Ages)

parasang an ancient Persian measure of distance estimated at about 5.6 kilometers

parascience science that is not mainstream; science pursued supplementally

parasomnia any of several sleep disorders, such as sleepwalking or doing other things while asleep

Parasqualodon extinct genus of toothed whale from 30 million years BCE

Paratethys Sea a large, shallow sea (at times a megalake) historically stretching from the Alps to Central Asia – the Black, Caspian, and Aral Seas are remnants

parthian shot a hostile, departing remark; [*Parthians* were archers known for firing arrows whilst in retreat (or pretending to retreat)]

parvenu (feminine: *parvenue*) one who has suddenly risen to a monied or powerful life-position and has not yet acquired the manner commonly associated with that position; [French]

parvis cathedral front courtyard or church porch

pash a romantic infatuation, esp. a brief one; to kiss or snog; [predominantly British slang]

Pashupatastra weapon of the Hindu god Shiva (and other deities) capable of destroying all creation and discharged by mind, eyes, words, or bow

pataphysics the pseudo-scientific or philosophical study of imaginary phenomena that may exist beyond metaphysics; the science of imaginary solutions; [from French writer Alfred Jarry 1873–1907]; [adj. *pataphysical*]

Pavlopetri the oldest (about 5000 years) known submerged lost city in the Mediterranean Sea; [Greek *Paul's stone*]

pavonine characteristic of a peacock, esp. its colorful tail; iridescent

pawn storm a coordinated attack using several pawns – a tactic in chess

Peaches of Immortality peaches, the eating of which grant immortality – from a tree that produces leaves once every millennium and fruits once in four; [Chinese myth.]

peahen (masculine: *peacock*) female peafowl

pellock a porpoise

pellucid perfectly clear; transparent; limpid;
"Of all that is most beauteous – imaged there
In happier beauty; more *pellucid* streams,
An ampler ether, a diviner air,
And fields invested with purpureal gleams."
– William Wordsworth, 19th c. English poet

pelmatogram footprint, esp. taken as an imprint on paper or in plaster

pelves plural of pelvis

pendragon a chief or dictator; title bequeathed on a chief of chiefs in ancient Britain

penetralia the innermost recesses of any thing or place, esp. of a temple or palace; hidden things or secrets; sanctuary

pennipotent strong of wing; strong in flight; [Latin *penna* (wing) + *potens* (strong)]

penumbra a partial shadow, as in the margin of an eclipse; anywhere something exists to a lesser degree; any outlying and surrounding area

peradventure by chance; perhaps; it may be; if; supposing

perfervid very fervid; ardent; impassioned

peri a fairy in Persian myth.; a beautiful, graceful woman

periastron (pl. *periastrons* or *periastra*) the point when a celestial body is nearest the star it orbits; [Ancient Greek *perí* (around) + *ástron* (star)]

periblepsis the wild gaze that may accompany delirium

perihelion (pl. *perihelia*) nearest point in an object's orbit around the Sun

perijove point at which any Jovian moon is closest to Jupiter

perimortem near the time of death; [Ancient Greek *perí* (about, around)]

periplus a circumnavigation; an epic voyage around a sea or a land; an account of such a voyage

perlustrate to travel through and examine an area; to survey thoroughly

permyriad one out of every ten thousand

perpend ponder; to weigh carefully in the mind

persiflate to talk in a bantering way

pessimal bad to a maximal extent; worst; of an organism's environment, least conducive to survival; [noun: *pessimum*]

petrichor the distinctive scent of first rain after a dry spell; any post-rain smell of earth; [Greek *petra* (rock) + *ichor* (blood of the gods)]

Pett Bottom actual small English settlement near Canterbury where the fictional James Bond lived with his aunt after his parents died

phantasm or **phantasma** (pl. *phantasmata*) something imagined to be seen or visible that has no objective reality; an illusion; a phantom; a specter; [adj. *phantasmic*]

phantasmagoria a constantly shifting complex sequence of real and/or imagined figures, as if seen in a dream; [adj. *phantasmagoric*]

phasmophobia a fear of ghosts; "The dell was dank, and darkening – his acute *phasmophobia* allowed only the most unsettled repose."

philomuse a lover of poetry, literature, and the arts

phthartic deadly; destructive; [Greek *phthartikos* destructive]

picaresque like a rascal, rogue, or adventurer

picaroon a pirate, corsair, or plunderer; a pirate ship; a rogue; a picaro; [Spanish *pícaro* rogue]

Pierian having to do with poetry, the arts, or artistic inspiration; [in Greek myth. the *Pierian* Spring of Macedonia was sacred to the Muses];
"A little learning is a dang'rous thing;
Drink deep, or taste not the *Pierian* spring."
– Alexander Pope, 18th c. English poet

pilcrow a paragraph mark; ¶

piloerection hairs standing on end

pishogue (PIH-showg) sorcery; witchcraft; blackmagic; an incantation or spell; [Irish *piseog* witchcraft]

Planet Heights an Antarctic mountain range that includes individual landforms with names from astronomy or astrology

plangent having a loud, mournful sound

plapper to make a noise with the lips

plashy watery; full of puddles or pools; splashy

pleasance a secluded part of a garden

plectrum a pick used to pluck the strings of a musical instrument

pleroma state of perfect fullness, esp. of God's being; [Ancient Greek *plérōma* (fullness, a filling up)]

plexure network or that which is woven together; the act of weaving together, or interweaving

plighted promised or bound by a solemn pledge, as a *plighted* bride; [archaic]

Pluma porgy or **Pimento grunt** an Atlantic fish

plumbless incapable of being measured or sounded; unfathomable

pluterperfect or **pluperfect** more than perfect; "The *pluterperfect* imperturbability of the department of agriculture." – James Joyce, *Ulysses*

plutography writing or other coverage of the wealthy, esp. of their lavish lifestyles; [Ancient Greek *ploûtos* (wealth) + *gráphō* (to write)]

pluviophile someone who loves the rain

pogonion (puh-GO-knee-un) the most forward-projecting point on the human chin

Polyhymnia or **Polymnia** the Muse of sacred poetry, dance, and eloquence; [Greek myth.]; [Greek *poly* (many) + *hymnos* (praise)]

porpentine the porcupine

portolan a European navigational sailing chart with illustrations & notes on hazards, coasts, ports, etc.

postcenal after dinner

prajna wisdom or understanding; [Buddhism]

prana substance that originates from the sun, permeates all reality, and connects the elements; [Hindu philosophy]; [Sanskrit *breath, life*]

pranava one of many names for the meditative syllable *Om*, commonly used as a mantra; *pranava* refers to *Om* as the primeval sound; [Hinduism]

precariat the class of people suffering *precarity*; people living precarious lives, esp. without job security; [*precarious* + *proletariat*]

prelapsarian relating to before the Fall; Eden before the lost innocence of Adam and Eve; relating to any past period of carefree innocence; [Latin *pre* (before) + *lapsus* (fall)]

prelusive of the nature of a prelude; introductory; indicating that something of a like kind is to follow

Presqueillian a resident of Presque Isle, Maine

presque vu a feeling that you are on the edge of grasping something; having something on the *tip of your tongue*; [French *nearly seen*]

preta hungry ghosts that, due to bad karma (greed, etc.) in a previous life, return with an insatiable hunger for something, often feces or corpses; [Hindu & Buddhist lore]

preterhuman more than human; beyond what is commonly characteristic of a human

princesse lointaine an ideal but unattainable female love interest; [French *distant princess*]

princock a conceited young rogue

prinkling prickling; tingling; [Scottish]

procellous stormy; [Latin *procella* storm]

promethean of or pertaining to Prometheus; life-giving; inspiring; boldly creative;

"From women's eyes this doctrine I derive:
They sparkle still the right *Promethean* fire;
They are the books, the arts, the academes,
That show, contain, and nourish all the world."
– Shakespeare, *Love's Labour's Lost*

Prometheus in Greek myth, the Titan chained to Mount Caucasus by Zeus for giving fire (stolen from heaven) to mankind; also a moon of Saturn; [Ancient Greek *pró* (before) + *manthánō* (to think)]

prosody the study of meter and its structure in verse; the patterns of rhythm and sound in poetry

protogenesis theory that livings things can generate from inanimate matter

protogenic formed at the beginning; primary; primeval

protohistoric of or pertaining to the period (between prehistory & history) of a given human society or culture before writing was developed

protopunk that portion of rock music (from roughly the 1960's to the mid-70's) that formed the basis for the later punk rock movement that included David Bowie, the Kinks, and the Velvet Underground

Prufrockian weary, timid, indecisive, and regretful; relating to the T. S. Eliot poem *The Love Song of J. Alfred Prufrock* – published in 1915

psionics mental powers that control or affect matter, such as telekinesis; [adj. *psionic*]

psithurism the sound of wind in trees or of rustling leaves; a whispering sound; [derived from Ancient Greek *psíthuros* (whispering, scandalous)]

psychagogic attractive; encouraging; persuasive; leading the soul; [Ancient Greek *agōgós* leading]

psychical nomadism the practice of taking what one likes from a religious, political, or other type of system and not embracing or adhering to the unappealing parts

psychogenic originating in the mind or in mental or emotional conflict, rather than being of physiological origin – esp. relating to the cause of physical symptoms

psychopomp an entity that guides souls to the afterlife; [Ancient Greek *psūkhé* (soul) + *pompós* (conductor)]

ptarmic sneeze-inducing; [Ancient Greek *ptarmós* sneeze]

puckfist a puffball (type of fungus); a braggart; a miser

pudor an appropriate sense of modesty or shame;
"Woman, undoing with sweet *pudor* her belt of rushrope, offers her allmoist yoni to man's lingam."
– James Joyce, *Ulysses*

puella aeterna (masculine: *puer aeternus*) in Jungian psychology, the archetype of the forever child who refuses to grow up; [Latin *eternal girl*]

pullulate to swarm; to teem; to multiply abundantly

Punkeydoodles Corners a hamlet in Ontario, Canada; [possibly derived from a mispronunciation of the song *Yankee Doodle*]

purple passages or **purple patch** a particularly rich, ornate, or fanciful part of a written work

purpureal purple; "Dreamt beneath the twilight gleaming the spires' *purpureal* hues / do speak to the Muse..." – Robin Devoe, *Pale Western Star*

purpurescent tinged with purple

putrilage remnants of putrefaction or decay

pyrography the art of burning designs into wood, leather, etc.; [adj. *pyrographic*]

pyrostat a fire alarm; a thermostat designed for high temperatures

pythogenic produced by, or originating from, filth or garbage; [obsolete]

pythonic relating to divination; prophetic; like an oracle (or pythoness); python-like; huge; monstrous; [Greek *python* (spirit of divination)]

Q

qasida an elegiac or satirical Arabic poem

quaintrelle a female dandy; a woman focused on high fashion, style, and leisurely pursuits

quakebuttock a traitor; a coward

Quantrill's Raiders a pro-Confederate guerrilla group during the American Civil War that included famed outlaw Jesse James; [leader William *Quantrill*]

quartering searching for prey by traversing an area, such as dogs or raptors hunting for game

quarterpace a staircase platform where the stairs turn 90 degrees

queachy shaking; trembling or yielding underfoot, as boggy ground

quebrada a ravine or gorge, esp. in Latin America

quercine of or pertaining to oak trees

querencia an area in the bull-ring where the bull feels strong and safe

quersprung in skiing, a jumpturn in which the skis land at right angles to the poles

Questing Beast or **Beast Glatisant** from the Arthurian legend, a creature with head and neck of a snake, body of a leopard, haunches of a lion, and feet of a hart – makes a sound like many barking hounds; [French *glapissant* yelping]

quiddative relating to or containing the essence of a person or thing

quiddler one who wastes time; an idler or dawdler at work; esp. when such idling interferes with the work of others

R

rafty damp; muggy; musty; [British]

Ragnarök in Norse myth., a series of apocalyptic events incl. a great battle betweens gods, giants, and monsters; natural disasters; and water covering the Earth; [Old Norse *fate of the gods*]

rainbow bee-eater colorful Australian bird that can eat several hundred bees a day

Raindoor Pass a mountain pass in British Columbia

rakehell a lewd, dissolute fellow; a debauchee; a rake

ramagious wild; not tame; [obsolete]

Rama Setu or **Adam's Bridge** a 30-mile chain of limestone shoals between India and Sri Lanka that was probably a land bridge before the 15th century; [early Islamic texts describe Adam crossing the bridge to India from Eden]

ramfeezled tired; exhausted

rampallian a scoundrel; a wretch

rampasture a communal dorm room for unmarried men

rampick or **rampike** a standing dead tree, esp. a skeletal tree or a splintered trunk killed by wind, lightning, or fire

Rampisham Down a chalk hill in Dorset, England

rangiferine or **rangerine** relating to or akin to caribou or reindeer

Rannerdale Knotts a hill in the English Lake District

rantipole a wild, unruly, and rakish young person

rara avis a rare, unique, or extraordinary person or thing;
[Latin *rare bird*]

rataplan the iterative sound of beating a drum, or of
a galloping horse; any drumming sound;
"The *rataplan* of her aortal pulse..."
– Robin Devoe, *Dynasties of Artistic Woodland*

ravening eager for plunder; greedily devouring

reality tunnel the theory that due to subconscious
mental filters, arising from one's beliefs and
experiences, we each interpret the world differently

recherché sought out with care; choice; of rare quality,
elegance, or attractiveness; unique and refined; [French]

reckling a weak child or animal, esp. the weakest of the
brood or litter

reiver or **reaver** one who takes away by violence or
by stealth; a robber, pillager, or plunderer

rejectamenta things thrown away or rejected; garbage;
waste; ejecta

relucent reflecting light; shining; glittering; glistening;
bright; luminous; splendid

rememorative tending or serving to remind

Republic of the Isle of Roses an unrecognized micronation
consisting of a 400-square-meter man-made platform in
the Adriatic Sea – independence was declared May 1,
1968 and the platform was destroyed by the Italian Navy
less than a year later

Republic of Upingtonia a Boer republic from 1885-86 in
the area of present-day Namibia;
[Prime Minister *Upington* of Cape Colony]

retrophilia attracted to the past or preferring old-fashioned
things; [noun: *retrophile*]

revanche revenge; a nation's or ethnic group's political
policy of regaining lost territory; [adj. & noun: *revanchist*]

Revelstoke Mountain Resort ski resort with the most vertical descent (1710 meters) in North America; [*Revelstoke*, British Columbia, Canada]

revenant someone who returns from a long absence; a person or thing reborn; a supernatural being that comes back to life; a zombie or ghost

rhadamanthine stern and inflexibly just; uncompromising and severe in judgement; [after *Rhadamanthus* in Greek myth., ruler of the underworld and known for dispensing justice]

rhinocerotic of or pertaining to the rhinoceros

rivage shore or coast; "From the green *rivage* many a fall / Of diamond rillets musical" – Tennyson

rivel to contract into wrinkles; to shrivel; to shrink; a wrinkle; [verb & noun]

rosmarine a fabled, walrus-like, marine animal capable of climbing by means of its teeth to the tops of rocks to feed upon the dew

Rottenegg a village in Austria

Rough and Ready a town in northern California; [from a mining company named after President Zachary Taylor's nickname: "Old *Rough & Ready*"]

rubegoldbergian achieving an easy or simple goal in an absurdly complicated manner; describing something that is much more complicated or elaborate than it needs to be; [from *Rube Goldberg*, American cartoonist known for portraying unnecessarily complicated gadgets]

rudesby an uncivil, turbulent fellow

rufescent tinged red or reddish

Runeberg, Johan Ludvig a national poet of Finland celebrated on Runeberg Day (February 5th); [surname loosely translated *mountain of letters*]

Rupelian age between 33.9 and 28.1 million years BCE in the geologic timescale; [*Rupel*, a Belgian river]

Rupes Nigra a 16th century phantom island imagined to be located at the magnetic north pole; [Latin *black rock*]

rupicaprine relating to or akin to chamois, a southern European goat-antelope; [Latin *rupes* (cliff, rock) + *capra* (goat)]

rutilant having a reddish glow; shining; [verb: *rutilate*]

S

sables black clothes worn during mourning periods

sabrage the opening of a bottle by slicing off the bottle's neck with a saber sword; [French]

Sacred Band of Thebes a troop of elite soldiers in the Theban army that consisted of 150 pairs of male lovers (4th century BCE)

saeter or **shieling** a mountain meadow or pasture used seasonally for grazing; [Northern Europe]

Saharan Atlas Algerian mountain range that forms the northern edge of the Saharan Desert – part of the Atlas Mountain System

Saint Luke's summer a brief period of warm weather around St. Luke's Day – October 18; "Almost every virtue of every season is contracted into the little span of *St. Luke's summer*, the very vintage of the year's juices." – Sir William Beach Thomas, *The Yeoman's England*

salariat salary earners as a group or a class

salmanazar a Burgundy wine bottle holding the volume equivalent to about 12 normal bottles; [from the Assyrian king *Shalmaneser V*]

samodiva (pl. *samodivi*) in Slavic folklore, woodland fairies or nymphs with an affinity for fire and often depicted as ethereal, long-haired maidens in feathered white gowns; [*samodiva* has Indo-European roots meaning divinity, wild, or rave]

samphire name for several salt-tolerant succulents (halophytes); [corruption of French *Saint Pierre*]

samsara in Hinduism and Buddhism, the ongoing cycle of birth, death, and rebirth endured by human beings and all other mortal beings, and from which release is obtained by achieving the highest enlightenment

Sandalphon an archangel in Jewish and Christian writings who gathers prayers and passes them on to God – twin brother of the angel Metatron; [possibly derived from Greek *syn-* (together) + *adelphos* (brother)]

Sandman a mythical character that sprinkles magic sand or dust on the closed eyes of sleepers (esp. children) and inspires beautiful dreams; [European folklore]

sang froid or **sangfroid** level-headedness; composure; coolness in trying circumstances; [French *sang* (blood) + *froid* (cold)]

sanguifluous flowing with blood

sanguisugent blood-sucking

sapphic lesbian; [ancient Greek poet *Sappho* of the island Lesbos]

saprogenic causing or resulting from putrefaction or decay; [Greek *saprós* putrid]

saprostomous having bad breath; [rare]

sarcophile a carnivorous animal; [Ancient Greek *sárx* flesh]

sarcophilous or **sarcophagous** prone to eating flesh

sardanapalian decadently luxurious and effeminate; like *Sardanapalus* (a latter king of Assyria) in a Lord Byron play

sardonic derisive, mocking, malignant, or bitterly sarcastic; [after the Mediterranean island *Sardinia* – eating a Sardinian plant was believed to produce facial convulsions resembling maniacal laughter]

sarky sarcastic; [British slang]

sastrugi (singular: *sastruga*) ridges of irregular design in snow that run parallel to the prevailing wind

saturnalia a period or occasion of general license, in which the passions or vices are allowed riotous indulgence; a particularly riotous, and esp. a drink- or drug-heavy, party; [adj. *saturnalian*]; [from the ancient Roman festival of *Saturn* during which class distinctions, including slavery, were temporarily suspended]

Saturnian resembling a golden age of serenity and happiness; related to the planet Saturn; of or pertaining to Saturn (Roman god of agriculture); "Augustus, born to bring *Saturnian* times." – Alexander Pope, English poet

saturnine heavy; grave; gloomy; dull

satyaloka in Hindu myth., the highest heaven; [Sanskrit *world of truth*]

Saxemberg Island a phantom island in the South Atlantic supposedly sighted by several ships and having a central mountain feature – appeared on charts between the 17th and 19th centuries

scandent of plants, having a tendency to climb whilst growing; "Where the very lifestroke of all breathing nature softly wails / For a *scandent* Heaven whose silken strands enfill all space."
– Robin Devoe, *Deeping Legends of a Purple Land*

Scandia Scandinavia; [poetic]

scapegrace a rogue; a man or boy of reckless and unprincipled habits; an incorrigible scamp

Schmiergeld a bribe; [German *schmieren* (to bribe) + *Geld* (money)]

schnozzle or **schnozzola** or **schnozz** a human nose, esp. a large one; [Yiddish *shnoyts* snout]

schussboomer a fast and skilled downhill skier; [German *Schuss* (straight downhill ski run)]

schwerpunkt the focal point; a point of maximum effort, esp. in a military operation; [German *schwer* (weighty) + *Punkt* (point)]

scobiform resembling sawdust or wood scrapings; [Latin *scobis* sawdust]

scotophobia fear of the dark; [Ancient Greek *skótos* darkness]

screenland Hollywood; the film industry

scrippage the contents of a scrip, or wallet; baggage

scry to predict the future using crystal balls; descry

Sea Bound Coast, The a nickname for Nova Scotia

Sea Cloud a sailing yacht launched in 1931 – as of 2022, she's the world's oldest ocean-going passenger ship

seacock a daring sailor or rover of the seas; a valve in a ship's hull opened to let water in or to expel wastewater

sealine the horizon at sea; coastline

sea-morse the walrus

seapunk a fashion and visual arts style emphasizing aquatic themes and colors

sea smoke fog over the ocean, caused by cold air moving over warmer water

seastallion (feminine: *seamare*) a male seahorse

sea-unicorn the narwhal

secreta products of secretion, as by an organ

seif dune (sayf doon) a long, narrow sand dune – common in the Sahara; [Arabic *sayf* sword]

selcouth rarely known; unusual; strange; marvelous; [rare]; "'A *selcouth* novelty,' muttered the knight, 'to advance to storm such a castle without pennon or banner displayed.'" – Walter Scott, *Ivanhoe*

selenophile a lover of the Moon; [Ancient Greek *seléne* (moon) + *phílos* (beloved)]

selkie a creature that is seal-like in water, but human on land; [Celtic and Norse myth.]

selva a rainforest in a tropical area, esp. the Amazon basin; [Portuguese *selva* (jungle, forest)]

Semigallian an extinct Baltic language; [*Semigallians* – a Baltic tribe]

semiplume a bird feather with a plumelike web and the shaft of an ordinary feather

semispheric having the form of half a sphere

semitaur mythical creature that is half-man, half-bull

sempervirent evergreen; always fresh

sempiternal everlasting; endless; having beginning, but no end; eternal; "The story of Jesus is the *sempiternal* Cinderella story, lifted to cosmic dimensions." – H.L. Mencken, American journalist

sensiferous exciting or conveying sensation

sensorium (pl. *sensoria*) the whole sensory system of an organism; the part of the brain that receives stimuli; the seat of sensation; [Latin *sēnsōrium* (organ of sensation)]; "More lovely the setting could not be nor seem, as if our *sensoria* evolved to imbibe only the beautiful, only the pleasant..."

Sepharial *nom de plume* of Walter Gorn Old (1864-1929), an influential English astrologer; [*Sepharial*, an angel from the apocryphal *Book of Enoch*]

sepulchral of or pertaining to burial or the grave; funereal; gloomy; [Latin *sepulcrum* (tomb, grave)]

seraph (pl. *seraphim*) one of an order of celestial beings, each having three pairs of wings;
"As full, as perfect, in vile man that mourns,
As the rapt *seraph* that adores and burns." – Pope

seraphic of or relating to a seraph; pure; sublime; blissful; angelic; "Their passion seems to have been of the *seraphic* kind. She devoted herself to religion, and persuaded him to do the same."
– Thomas Pennant, 18th c. Welsh traveller & writer

serpentiferous featuring or bearing a snake; having many snakes

serpentry a winding motion like a serpent's; a place inhabited by serpents; snake-like behavior; collective term for all serpents

serpopard a mythical animal of ancient Egypt with a long neck and the head of a snake; also called *serpent-necked lion*; [*serpent* + *leopard*]

serried placed close together in rows, esp. soldiers placed in a grid pattern

Seventeen Seventy Australian town in Queensland named for the year Captain James Cook arrived

sexy prime a prime number that differs from another prime by six – e.g. 31 & 37; [Latin *sex* six]

Shambhala or **Shambala** a mythical kingdom from which a Bhudda, in 2424, will emerge with a large army to defeat evil powers and usher in a Golden Age; [Tibetan Buddhism]; [Sanskrit *śambhu* (existing for happiness)]

shambolic chaotic, disorganized, or mismanaged

Shangri-la a place of complete bliss, delight, and peace, esp. if also remote and isolated; paradise; [*Shangri* (an invented name in the novel *Lost Horizon*) + Tibetan *la* (a mountain pass)]

Sharanga the celestial bow of the Hindu god Vishnu

shellycoat a relatively harmless creature of myth with a coat of shells that rattle during movement – associated with rivers and streams; [Scotland & Northern England]

Shitlington Crags a rocky outcrop in Northern England

shivering owl a screech owl

shopdropping or **droplifting** covertly displaying objects in stores as a form of performance art

shot-clog a bore – tolerated because he or she buys drinks

shrike a predatory songbird; shriek

shrimping spooning, but in a pronounced fetal position

shrive to hear the confession of someone and give absolution

sialoquent tending to spray saliva during speech; [Ancient Greek *síalon* (spittle) + eloquent]

Sierra Sierra Delta Delta same sh*t, different day; [NATO phonetic alphabet]

sigmoid or **sigmoidal** curved like the letter C; crescent-shaped; curved like the letter S

sillage the trail of scent left by someone's perfume; [French *wake* or *trail*]; "She could follow him blind, so thick and sickening his *sillage* lay..."

Silurian of the geologic period 439-409 million years BCE – when the first terrestrial plants appeared

silva or **sylva** the forest trees of a region or country, considered collectively; a description or history of the forest trees of a country; [Latin *silva* forest]

silvan or **sylvan** pertaining to the forest or woodlands;
   residing in a forest; covered in forest;
   "Thou still unravish'd bride of quietness,
   Thou foster-child of silence and slow time,
   Sylvan historian, who canst thus express
   A flowery tale more sweetly than our rhyme:
   What leaf-fringed legend haunts about thy shape?"
   – John Keats, 19th c. English Romantic poet
Silverpilen a Stockholm ghost train featured in several
   urban legends; [Swedish *silver arrow*]
Silvretta Montafon large Austrian ski area
simoon a strong, hot, sandy wind in Arabia or Northern
   Africa; [Arabic *samūm* (hot wind))]
singultus a hiccup; [Latin *speech interrupted by sobs*]
Sinthgunt in German myth., a goddess with healing powers,
   attested in the Merseburg Incantation – two magic spells
   written in Old High German circa 1000 CE;
   [possibly derived from Germanic roots meaning
   the night-walking one]
sirenic or **sirenical** alluring and/or tempting, esp.
   dangerously so; melodious; [from *sirens*, creatures
   that lured sailors with lovely song to shipwreck on
   their island's rocky coast]; [Greek myth.]
sirocco an oppressive, hot wind, esp. one from the Libyan
   deserts felt in southern Europe; [Italian *scirocco*]
sistren sisters; the feminine form of brethren
sistrum (pl. *sistra*) an ancient Egyptian percussive musical
   instrument
sitzfleisch the ability to endure or carry on with an activity;
   [German *sitzen* (to sit) + *Fleisch* (flesh)]
sitzkrieg a non-shooting war; wartime without violence;
   cold war; [German S*itzkrieg* (sitting war)]
sitzpinkler an unmanly man; a man dominated by his wife
   or girlfriend; [German, literally: *a man who pees sitting
   down*]

six nines in pi the decimal representation of the number pi happens to include six 9's in a row after the 762nd decimal point

skald Scandinavian bard of the Viking era; [adj. *skaldic*]

Skidbladnir in Norse myth., a ship crafted by two dwarfs that could carry all the gods, always had a favorable wind, and could collapse to pocket size

skinwalker a person that can transform into any animal by wearing its pelt; [Native American myth.]

skirl to produce a shrill sound, like that of bagpipes

skookum excellent; high quality; impressive; strong; durable; [British Columbia, Yukon, and NW U.S.]

Skraelings the name Norse Greenlanders historically used for native peoples in Canada and Greenland; [Old Norse *skrá* (dried skin) – in reference to Inuit animal pelts]

skyclad being naked outdoors; [poetic]

skyquakes unexplained sounds heard in various places world-wide – similar to thunder, cannon fire, or sonic booms

skysill the horizon; [poetic]

skyspace room designed with an opening to the sky

slade a little dell or valley

Sleaford Mere a permanent saline lake in southern Australia; [Old English *sliow* & *ford* (ford over a slimy river) + *mere* (lake)]

sleech slimy mud or sludge; a coastal mudflat; [UK]; "Please remove your *sleechy* boots afore entry."

Sleipnir (slayp-neer) the Norse god Odin's 8-legged horse

slickenside in geology, a rock surface polished smooth by friction or produced from cleavage

sloom a gentle or light sleep; slumber; [adj. *sloomy*]

slumberland fanciful place where everyone is asleep

slumberous inviting slumber; soporiferous; being in the repose of slumber; sleepy; drowsy; "Pensive in the *slumberous* shade." – Alexander Pope

slummock to lumber; to walk with heavy and awkward movements; to behave lazily; a slovenly individual; [verb & noun]

slurvian speech, esp. English speech, that is notably slurred or sloppily pronounced; a colloquial version of a language noted by slurred or carelessly combined words; [informal]

smeeth to smooth; to blacken with smoke; [British]

smokefall the end of day before nightfall, when fog comes;
"But only in time can the moment in the rose-garden,
The moment in the arbour where the rain beat,
The moment in the draughty church at *smokefall*
Be remembered; involved with past and future."
– T.S. Eliot

sniggler someone who fishes for eels

snowbroth snow and water mixed; very cold liquor

Snowdonia a mountainous region of northwest Wales

snowdrop windflower white-flowered Eurasian herb

snuffle breathing noisily through a partially blocked nose

snuggery a snug, cozy place

softscape the living, cultivated flora of a landscape, such as shrubbery and flowers

solastalgia type of homesickness experienced while still at home, but when the natural or built environment has changed; [Latin *sōlācium* (solace) + *-algia* (pain) – coined by Australian philosopher Glenn Albrecht]

solisequious (adj.) following the course of the sun, esp. describing plants; [Latin *sol* (sun) + *sequor* (I follow)]

solivagant wandering alone; a solo wanderer; [adj. & noun]

soma ritual drink in ancient Vedic culture; any intoxicating drug; a contentment drug in Aldous Huxley's novel *Brave New World*; the corporeal human body; [Ancient Greek *sôma* body]

somnolescent half-asleep; sleepy

Somnus Roman god of sleep – his father is Night and his twin is Death

sophianic having to do with wisdom; like wisdom;
   [Greek *sophos* wise]
soulcraft a soul-nourishing or soul-shaping activity
soundwalk an excursion the main purpose of which is to
   take in the sounds of the environment
southern cassowary a flightless black bird (second heaviest
   in the world) of Indonesia, Papua New Guinea, and
   northeastern Australia – sometimes called the world's
   most dangerous bird, but human deaths resulting from
   its powerful kick and blade-like claws are rare
Southern Local Supervoid an almost empty region of
   space near our galaxy and 600 billion times its size
Southern Owl Nebula a symmetric, nearly round nebula in
   the constellation Hydra
spadassin swordsman; [French *spada* sword]
Spandaramet goddess of death and the underworld;
   [Armenian myth.]
spectrophobia a morbid fear of mirrors or of one's own
   reflection
spiloma a mole; a birthmark; a naevus
spilth a spillage; spilled material
spirituelle having an ethereal nature; refined; pure
spizzerinctum nerve; guts; zeal; determination; ardor
splanchnic visceral; intestinal
splattergun a shotgun; any gun that fires quickly and
   somewhat inaccurately
spoondrift or **spindrift** water sprayed into the air by wind
   at sea; snow blowing off mountain peaks
sprezzatura performing a difficult task with grace and ease;
   effortlessness; nonchalance; esp. used to describe art or
   an artistic method; [Italian *sprezzatura* nonchalance]
spumescent resembling froth or foam; foaming
sputative inclined to expectorate; spitting frequently
squamulose covered with small scales (fish, reptiles, fungi,
   or plants); [Latin *squamula* (small scales)]

squillion a large, indeterminate number, often used hyperbolically; "There were about seventy-nine *squillion* people in the world, and if you were very lucky, you would end up being loved by fifteen or twenty of them."
– Nick Hornby, English writer

squitters loose, watery stools; "Suffering a dire case of the *squitters*, she was wise to skip the opera."

squitter-wit a person who writes worthless prose

St Ninian's Isle Treasure a 28-piece hoard of early medieval silver metalwork discovered by a schoolboy in Scotland in 1958

starcraft astrology

starko naked; [British slang]

steampunk a science fiction subgenre depicting advanced technologies usually set in an anachronistic Victorian era

stelliferous having, or abounding with, stars

stillicide water dripping, esp. from stalactites, icicles, or the eave of a roof

stinkhorn a type of fungus

stonedelf (pl. *stonedelves*) a quarry of rock or stone

stonepit a quarry

stonking awesome or amazing; powerful; [British slang]

strange-tailed tyrant South American bird with a curiously-shaped tail of the family Tyrannidae

stravage stroll; meander; roam; wander; [Scotland & Ireland]

stridulate to make a shrill or musical sound, like the males of many insects; [adj. *stridulous*]

sturmfrei having the house to oneself, as when parents or flatmates are away; [German S*turm* (storm) + *frei* (free)]

stygian of or relating to the Styx, one of five rivers of hell; infernal; dark and gloomy; "Her genuflective orison rolls across the acheronian moor,
into the spume, and on
for the far, *stygian* shore."
– Robin Devoe, *Lady o' the Loch*

subboreal very cold

subcelestial beneath the heavens; terrestrial

subderisorious ridiculing in a loving manner; ridiculing with moderation or delicacy; [obsolete]

subdulcid slightly sweet; somewhat sweet

subnascent growing underneath

subnivean of or living in the air space between the ground and snow; [noun: *subnivium*]

subnubilar under clouds

subterfluent running under or beneath; [rare]

subxeric describing an extremely dry region

sunstrike a blinding glare from the sun, esp. if driving

suntrap a place that captures the heat of the sun

supercrescent growing on something else that is also growing

superjacent positioned immediately above or on top of something else; overlying

supernatant floating on the surface of a liquid

supersensible or **supersensual** spiritual; beyond the reach of the human senses

surquedry or **surquidry** overweening pride; arrogance; [obsolete]; [Old French *surcuiderie*]

susurrous whispering; rustling; full of whispering, hissing, or murmuring sounds; [noun: *susurration*];
"Halleck nodded, heard the faint *susurration* and felt the air shift as a lockport swung open beside him."
– Frank Herbert, *Dune*

susurrus a whispering or rustling sound; a murmur;
"The soft *susurrus* and sighs of the branches."
– Longfellow

swaddled babies a common name for *anguloa uniflora*, an orchid native to the Andes region

swale a tract of low, usually wet land; a drainage ditch

Sweet Swan of Avon, the a moniker for playwright William Shakespeare; [poetic]

sweven a vision; a dream; [Old English *swefn* (sleep, dream)]

sybilline or **sibylline** of or pertaining to a sibyl (a female oracle); having oracle-like powers of prediction; clairvoyant; mysterious; cryptic

sylph an elemental being of air, usually female; a slender woman, esp. a graceful and sublime one; [Latin *sylvestris* (of the woods) + *nympha* (nymph)]

sylvestral of, pertaining to, similar to, or growing in trees or forests

synaesthesia a psychological process wherein one senses something in terms of another sense, e.g. hears a color or sees a sound; an artistic device wherein one sense is described in terms of another; "Into her darkness, a churning *synaesthesia,* where her pain was the taste of old iron, scent of melon, wings of a moth brushing her cheek." – William Gibson, *Neuromancer*

syrinx a set of pan-pipes; the vocal organ of birds; a narrow channel cut in rock

syrt a quicksand or bog; [Ancient Greek *Súrtis* (name of sandbanks off the Libyan coast)]

T

tachyonic antitelephone a hypothetical device once theorized (by Einstein and others) to be capable of sending signals into one's own past

Taklamakan Desert a shifting sand desert nearly Germany's size located in northwestern China; [wrongly thought to mean "place you enter, but never leave," the name likely means "abandoned place" or "place of ruins"]; [Persian *makan* place]

talaria the winged, golden sandals of the messenger gods Hermes and Mercury; [Greek & Roman myth.]; [Latin *talaris* (pertaining to ankle or heel)]

tanglery the upper regions of a dense forest, esp. a rainforest, where the branches and leaves of trees and other foliage intertwine

Tango Uniform broken beyond repair; dead; [from military slang "toes up" and *T* & *U* of the NATO phonetic alphabet]

Tantalus for stealing ambrosia and nectar from the gods at Olympus, Tantalus is forever cursed to stand in a pool of water beneath boughs of fruit – yet never able to slake his thirst or satisfy his hunger; [Greek myth.]

Tanzania a country in East Africa that includes Africa's highest peak, Mount Kilimanjaro; [1964 union of former republics *Tanganyika* & *Zanzibar*]

tarasque a dragon-like mythical creature with a leonine head, a turtle-like carapace, six feet with ursine claws, a scaly tail, and poisonous breath; [southern France]

tardigrade sluggish; slow in movement; a sloth; a phylum of 8-legged micro-animals, AKA water bears or moss piglets; [adj. & noun]; [Latin *tardus* (slow) + *gradior* (walk)]

Tardis Chasma a canyon-like feature on Charon, a satellite of dwarf planet Pluto; [from *TARDIS* (**T**ime **A**nd **R**elative **D**imension **I**n **S**pace) in the British TV series *Doctor Who*]

Tatzelwurm in folklore of the Alps, a multi-legged lizard up to 7 feet in length with the face of a cat and poisonous breath – may emit shrieks, hisses, or whistles; [German *Tatze* (claw) + *Wurm* (worm)]

telluric terrestrial; pertaining to the Earth

temerarious reckless; rash; dangerously bold in action; [Latin *temerē* (by chance, rashly)]

Tempean beautiful and charming, as in scenery or landscape; [from *Tempe*, a valley in northern Greece celebrated by ancient poets for its beauty]

temulent drunk; intoxicated

Tengerism an ancient Central Asian religion based on animism & shamanism – centered on the sky god *Tengri*; [derived from an old Turkic word for dawn]

Terra Nivium a triangular highland region on the Moon; [Latin *Land of Snows*]

terrigenous Earthborn; produced by the Earth; in geology, derived from erosion of land-based rocks

tessellated covered with similarly shaped pieces; decorated with pieces of glass or stone like a mosaic; checkered

tesseract a 4-dimensional cube; [mathematics]

tetracontagon a 40-sided polygon

tetragrammaton any four-letter word

tetralemma a perplexity with four possible alternatives

tetramerous consisting of four parts, esp. in botany

thalassic of or relating to seas and oceans; [Ancient Greek *thálassa* sea]

thalassophile someone who loves the sea or ocean

thanatoid resembling death; seemingly dead; deadly; [Ancient Greek *thánatos* death]

thanatophilia a love of death; a deep fascination with death

thanatopsis (pl. *thanatopses*) contemplation of death; title of poem by William Cullen Bryant; [Ancient Greek *thánatos* (death) + *ópsis* (seeing)]

Thanatos god of death; twin of Hypnos (god of sleep); [Greek myth.]

theopathy the emotional experience arising from religious belief; [adj. *theopathic*]

theopoetic related to theopoetics, an inter-disciplinary field of study combining aspects of poetic analysis, religious belief, and postmodern philosophy; "Her sublime verse, steeped in *theopoetic* sentiment, inspired generations of sensitive seekers of the Divine."

theory of everything a hypothetical, singular theoretical framework of physics that explains all aspects of the physical universe

thermoluminescence when certain crystalline materials release previously absorbed energy as light

Theron Mountains a mountain group in Antarctica

Thesan in Etruscan myth., goddess of the dawn; [Etruscan *thesan* (dawn, divination)]

Thespis an ancient Greek poet, traditionally credited with inventing Greek tragedy; [adj. *thespian*]

Thirty Thousand Islands the world's largest freshwater archipelago located in Georgian Bay, Lake Huron, Ontario

threnody an ode or song of lament; a dirge; [adj. *threnodic*]; [Ancient Greek *thrēnōidía* lamentation]

thunderboomer a large, dynamic thunderstorm

thunder-box portable lavatory

thunderstone a thunderbolt; any of the various stones regarded in some myths as having been cast to the earth as thunderbolts, such as meteorites and some ancient artifacts

thunderworm a burrowing, snake-like lizard native to Florida; [leaves its burrow after thunderstorms]

thyrsus (pl. *thyrsi*) a pinecone-tipped, ivy-entwined staff carried by Dionysus and his followers

tiggerish energetic & cheerful; [from *Tigger*, a character in English author A. A. Milne's Winnie-the-Pooh stories]

Tír na nÓg one of the names of the Celtic Otherworld, home to the deities and possibly the dead; an island paradise of everlasting youth, beauty, abundance, and joy; [Irish *Land of the Young*];
"But listen well. In *Tír na nÓg*, because there is no sorrow, there is no joy. Do you hear the meaning of the seachain's song?" – Alexandra Ripley, American novelist

Toad Suck a town in central Arkansas, USA

Torngat Mountains a mountain range in northeastern Canada; [derived from Inuktitut language (place of evil spirits)]

Torschlusspanik the sense that time is running out due to age, esp. a woman getting too old for childbirth; [German *gate-shut panic*]

tourbillion a vortex; a whirlwind; [French *tourbillon* whirlwind]

tovarish or **tovarisch** comrade; [Russian]

Tramontane or **tramontane** classical name for a northern wind; anything that comes from the other side of mountains, esp. from north of the Alps; anything foreign, strange, or barbarous; [Italian *tramontana* (beyond the mountains)]

transhumance the seasonal migration of livestock (with herders) between two regions

translunary being or lying beyond the Moon; ethereal; spiritual

transmarine lying or being beyond the sea; originating from across the sea

transpontine of, pertaining to, or situated on the far side of a bridge; of or pertaining to the sensational melodramas presented on the south side of the Thames in the 19th century or earlier

transvolation the act of flying beyond or across

treppenwitz a devastating rejoinder conceived only after leaving the place of debate; l'esprit d'escalier; afterwit; [German *Treppe* (stairs, steps) + *Witz* (wit)]

triffid a plant growing or spilling beyond normal bounds and seeming to overrun anything near by; anything that behaves in like manner; [*triffids*, a poisonous, mobile plant species in the 1951 novel *The Day of the Triffids*]

trigon a triangle; an ancient type of Oriental harp

trilemma a quandary having three possible choices

triquetrous three-sided; triangular; having three corners

Trisectrix of Maclaurin in geometry, a cubic plane curve that can be used to trisect an angle; [Colin *Maclaurin*, 18th c. Scottish mathematician]

tristesse sadness; misery; [adj: *tristful*]; [French]; [literary]

Troutbeck Tongue a small fell (or hill) in the English Lake District, the top of which affords a view of Windermere – England's largest natural lake

Truth or Consequences a town in the US state of New Mexico with hot springs; [renamed from Hot Springs in 1950 after a radio show contest]

tungsten or **wolfram** a rare metal with the highest melting point after carbon; [Swedish *tungsten* (heavy stone); German *wolf rahm* (wolf foam)]

Tunguska event, the a very large explosion (likely a meteoroid's air burst) in 1908 over Siberia that felled 80 million trees over 200 square kilometers

tunica intima the innermost layer of a blood vessel, such as an artery or vein; [New Latin *inner coat*]

turtling or **turning turtle** turning upside down, esp. floating craft; failing; going belly up; "The storm-*turtled* boats were soon righted and repaired."

twee overly quaint, dainty, cute, or nice; [British – from a child's pronunciation of sweet]

twitten a narrow passage between two hedges; [UK]

twitterlight twilight; "Cycling the fringe of that land's blue dream a rider alone could feel the mysterious, powerful love of the western horizon's *twitterlight* as a presence most palpable." – Robin Devoe, *The Season of Light*

tyrian a shade of purple; [from a dye rendered from mollusks in ancient *Tyre* (in modern Lebanon)]

U

ubermensch superman; a person with great powers; [German *over man*]

ugglesome horrible; gruesome

ullage the amount which a vessel, such as a cask, of liquor lacks of being full; wantage; deficiency; the amount (esp. of wine) abandoned unconsumed in glasses

Ultima Thule the end of the world; the last extremity; [Latin *ultimus* (furthest) + *Thule* (a legendary northern island)]

ultramontane being beyond or from beyond a mountain range, esp. the Alps

ultramundane extraordinary; extraterrestrial

ultrazodiacal outside the zodiac; being in part of the sky more than 8 degrees from the ecliptic, or the apparent annual path of the sun

umami (u-mah-mee) one of the five basic tastes – the savory taste of foods such as seaweed, cured fish, aged cheeses, and certain meats (the classic four tastes are sweet, sour, bitter, and salty); [Japanese *umami* sumptuousness]

umbles entrails, esp. those of a deer

umbra the darkest part of a shadow; a dark area; [adj. *umbral*]

umbramancy divination through the use of shadows

umbratic or **umbratical** of or relating to the shade or darkness; shadowy

umbratile a person who frequents the shadows or dark places; shady; shadowy; [noun & adj.]

umbriferous casting shade; umbrageous

Umwelt (pl. *umwelten*) a person's or organism's surrounding environment; [German *environment*]

underbreath a soft voice; a whisper; baseless rumor

undercast complete cloud cover below an observer

Undercliff, the several areas of landslip on England's southern coast

undercroft a cellar; a subterranean room of any kind, esp. one under a church or having a sacred purpose; a vault or secret walk underground

underdolven or **underdelved** past participle of underdelve, to dig down or under

undergear underwear

underlife the secret aspects of a person's life

underpuppy a small or insignificant underdog

undersong an accompanying sound; an underlying idea or atmosphere; an undertone

unreeve to withdraw or remove, as a rope from an opening

untreasure to bring forth; to give up, as things previously treasured; to remove, steal, or destroy treasure; "The quaintness with which he *untreasured*, as by rote, the stores of his memory." – John Mitford, 19th c. British journalist

ur- prefix meaning original, primitive, or first – as *ur*-myth or *ur*-poem; [similar usage to *proto*-]

urgrund basis, foundation, cause, or factor; a primal cause or ultimate cosmic principle; [German *ur*- (primal) + *Grund* (ground)]

urman coniferous forest; swampy Siberian forest

urtext original version of a literary or musical work

Useless Loop a town in western Australia

utopiate a drug that provides an escape from everyday life or generates idealistic dreams of utopia; [utopia + opiate – coined by a Stanford professor in 1964]

V

Valdivian temperate rain forest an ecoregion on the west coast of southern South America (Chile and Argentina); [*Valdivia*, a city in Chile]

Valkyrie in Norse myth., any female attendant of Odin that also guides fallen warriors from the battlefield to Valhalla; [adj. *Valkyrian*]; [Old Norse *valkyrja* (chooser of the slain)]

vaporetto (pl. *vaporetti*) motorboat used as a public waterbus on the canals of Venice, Italy

Varsovian of or pertaining to Warsaw, Poland; [Latin *Varsovia* Warsaw]

vastity emptiness or desolation; vastness, vastitude

vatic prophetic; pertaining to a prophet; oracular

Veblen good a luxury good, such as some cars, the demand of which increases, instead of decreases, as price increases – contradicting the law of demand; [American economist Thorstein *Veblen*]

vega a moist & fertile plain, esp. in Latin America; [Spanish]

Vela a constellation in the southern sky; [Latin *the sails*]

veldt or **veld** the open pastureland or grassland of South Africa; [Afrikaans]

velivolant flying with sails; passing under full sail

velleity the lowest degree of desire or volition, with no attendant effort toward action; a slight wish not followed by any effort to obtain; [Latin *velle* (to wish)]

Velvet Divorce the 1993, self-determined split of Czechoslovakia into Czech Republic and Slovakia; [from the bloodless *Velvet* Revolution (1989)]

ventripotent fat; gluttonous; having a large appetite; eating with greedy delight

vernalagnia the heightening of sexual desire or romantic feelings in springtime

Verona Rupes 12-mile high cliff (tallest in the Solar System) on Uranus's moon Miranda; [*Verona* (city of Romeo & Juliet) + Latin *rūpēs* (cliff)]

veronica in bullfighting, a slow circular movement of the cape away from a charging bull; [from the supposed similarity to how Saint *Veronica* held out a cloth to Christ]

versant the slope of a mountain or mountain ridge; the overall slope of a region

vertiginous having an aspect of great depth, drawing the eye to look downwards; inducing a feeling of giddiness, vertigo, or whirling; pertaining to vertigo; revolving

vespering (adj.) moving westward or toward the sunset; westering; [poetic]

vespertide or **eventide** evening

vespertine of, related to, or occurring in the evening

Vesuvian of or relating to Italian Mount Vesuvius – it erupted in 79 CE and buried Pompeii; prone to any type of sudden and explosive outburst

Victoriapeak an exoplanet orbiting the star Lionrock in the constellation Aquarius; [*Victoriapeak* and *Lionrock* are named after Hong Kong hills]

vigintillion an extremely large number; ten to the 63rd power

Vinland area of eastern Canada (including Newfoundland) named by Leif Erikson when vikings landed circa 1000 CE; [Old Norse *Vínland* (either Wineland or Meadowland)]

virago a woman of great stature, strength, and courage; a masculine woman; a female warrior

virga (pl. *virgae* or *virgas*) a visible streak of rain or snow that evaporates before reaching the ground; [Latin *virga* (rod, streak)]

Virgo Stellar Stream or **Virgo Overdensity** a small galaxy of a few hundred thousand stars orbiting (and likely eventually merging with) our galaxy

viripotent (of men) sexually fit and mature; reproductively able; generally marriageable

virtu a love of, knowledge of, or taste for objects of fine art; objects of art collectively

vituperate to overwhelm with wordy abuse; to censure severely; [adj. *vituperative* & *vituperable*]

vizard or **vizzard** a mask worn to disguise or protect the face; a pretense; [archaic];
"Oh, that deceit should steal such gentle shapes,
And with a virtuous *vizard* hide foul guile!"
– Shakespeare, *Richard III*

vocable able to be spoken; a word considered as sound only, without meaning; [adj. & noun];
"Without words and almost with the seriousness of asylum nurses they at once set upon an unsavoury-looking matron who began to cry out Mediterranean *vocables* of distress." – Anthony Burgess

volitive of or relating to the will or volition; emanating from the will; having the power to will; expressing a wish

volplane a steep, controlled dive, esp. by an aircraft with the engine off; the act of so diving; [French *vol* (flight) + *plané* (gliding)]

vomitorium (pl. *vomitoria*) a place where vomiting occurs; an exit from an amphitheatre

voortrekker a Boer (or Afrikaner) pioneer, who trekked from Cape Colony into the hinterland of what is now South Africa to establish the Transvaal and the Orange Free State during the 1830's

vorago abyss; chasm; gulf; [Latin]

vorpal sharp or deadly; [Lewis Carroll's poem *Jabberwocky*]

votive given in fulfillment of a vow

vulgus the common people; the public; a throng or crowd; [Latin]

W

Waldsterben the destruction of the forest caused by environmental pollution; [German *dying of the forest*]

wanderword a word that has spread to wide usage in many languages

wanweird an unhappy fate; [Scots *wan-* (bad) + *weird* (fate)]

Watch Croft a prominent hill in Cornwall, England

water chevrotain or **fanged deer** an ungulate of tropical Africa – largest of the 10 extant species of chevrotains, which as a group are the smallest hoofed mammals in the world, roughly dog-sized

weald a wood or forest; a wooded land or region

weathergleam clear sky upon the horizon; [Scottish]

weephole a small drainage opening in a wall

welkin the visible regions of the air; the vault of heaven; the sky; the firmament; the region above the clouds; "When storms the *welkin* rend."
– William Wordsworth, English Romantic poet

welter to tumble about, esp. in anything foul or defiling; to wallow; to rise and fall, as waves;
"When we *welter* in pleasures and idleness, then we eat and drink with drunkards." – Latimer;
"The *weltering* waves." – Milton

wester to move or turn to the west; a strong west wind, esp. a storm-bringing one; [verb & noun];
"The hills rose scarlet and gold to the north of the little town, and the *westering* sun shone ruddily and mystically..." – H. P. Lovecraft

wheep the sound of a weapon, esp. a sword, when drawn from its sheath

wheeple to whistle ineffectually

whicker to neigh; to laugh in a partially suppressed way

whistle pig the hoary marmot

white knighting defending someone unnecessarily, or to curry their favor

Whitney umbrella a particular three-dimensional, self-intersecting surface – the union of all straight lines passing through points of a fixed parabola (and adhering to three more criteria); [20th c. American mathematician Hassler *Whitney*]

widdendream or **widdrim** a mental state of confusion or extreme excitement; a blind fury; an insane outburst; [Scottish from Old English]

widdershins or **withershins** counterclockwise; moving in a counterclockwise or contrary direction; unlucky

wildered bewildered; perplexed;
"Again the *wildered* fancy dreams
Of spouting fountains, frozen as they rose..."
– William Cullen Bryant, 19th c. American Romantic poet

Wild's Triplet three interacting spiral galaxies 200 million light-years from Earth with luminous connecting bridges; [Australian astronomer Paul *Wild*]

windflaw a strong gust of wind

winterbourne a stream or spring that flows only in winter or only after rains

Winterval the period of holidays celebrated in many countries in midwinter

wispen (adj.) composed of wisps – slender flexible structures, esp. of cloud, smoke, or hair;
"Upon not a few Romantic landscapes she lingered, to wonder at the palette such a painter could pull – the perfect sky-borne hue of dying sun on cirrus *wispen*."
– Robin Devoe, *The Dreaming Spire*

Wolfenstein, the a rock formation in Bavaria, Germany consisting of granite blocks

wonderwork a wonderful work or act; miracle; thaumaturgy; "*Wonderworks* of God and Nature's hand." – Lord Byron, English Romantic poet

woodkern a thief who frequents forested areas

woodnote a song or call like that of a forest bird; natural, spontaneous musical note or song;
"So you'll live, you'll live, Young Fellow My Lad
In the gleam of the evening star,
In the *wood-note* wild and the laugh of the child, In all sweet things that are." – Robert Service

woodreeve the steward of a forested area

wordbound hindered by speech, esp. when too self-conscious of word usage to allow free expression

World Islands, The 300 small artificial islands positioned in the shape of a world map off the coast of Dubai and totaling 144 miles of shoreline

wunderpus octopus *Wunderpus photogenicus* lives in shallow waters of SE Asia and avoids predation by changing color and shape to mimic other sealife; [German *wunder* (wonder) + octopus]

wyvern a mythical creature resembling a dragon but with only two legs and a barbed tail

X

Xanadu the summer capital of Kublai Khan's empire; any beautiful and wondrous place

xenoarchaeology a hypothetical scientific discipline that studies the remains of alien cultures on planets inhabited or visited (usually long ago)

xenomorphic having a strange form; [noun: *xenomorph*]

xenophilia an attraction or love of foreign people, manners, or culture; [Ancient Greek *xénos* alien]

xerothermic dry and hot; [Ancient Greek *xērós* dry]

Xibalba Underworld ruled by 12 death lords and partially protected by rivers of scorpions, blood, and pus; [Mayan myth.]

Xiphodon an extinct camel-like animal

xiphoid process a small, vaguely sword-shaped, cartilaginous extension of the lower sternum

xylomancy divination using pieces of burning wood; [Ancient Greek *xúlon* (wood) + *manteía* (divination)]

Y

yarak in falconry, a super-alert state where the bird is hungry (but not weak) and ready to hunt; [Persian *yârakî* (power, strength, boldness)]

Yggdrasil the central, sacred ash tree in Norse cosmology, around which everything exists, including the nine worlds – a dragon/serpent gnaws at one of Yggdrasil's three roots and the tree's dew has sustaining powers

ylem (EE-lem) in cosmology, the primordial matter of the universe which existed before the Big Bang and creation of the elements; [Latin *hylem* matter]

Ymir (ee-mir) a primordial being in Norse myth. – three giants fashioned earth from Ymir's flesh; ocean from his blood; hills from his bones; plants from his hair; heavens from his skull; and clouds from his brain; also *Ymir* is a moon of Saturn

yokefellow or **yokemate** a partner; a work associate; a mate

Z

zaftig (ZOFF-tig) (of a woman) full-bosomed; having a plump and sexually attractive figure; voluptuous; well-proportioned; [Yiddish *zaftik* (juicy, succulent)]

zappy lively; energetic; entertaining

zarzuela a comic Spanish operetta

zazzy flashy; shiny; stylish; [slang]

Zealandia a mass of continental crust about half the size of Australia that broke away from the supercontinent Gondwanaland 23 million years BCE and was 94% submerged – New Zealand is the largest section that remains above sea level

zeitgeber a rhythmically occurring environmental cue, such as a change in light or temperature, that helps regulate an organism's biological clock; [German *Zeit* (time) + *Geber* (giver)]

zeitgeist (pl. *zeitgeisten*) the spirit of the age; the taste, outlook, and spirit characteristic of a particular era; [German *Zeit* (time) + *Geist* (spirit)]

Zelig one who naturally mimics those around him or her; one who changes his or her appearance to suit the surroundings; an unimportant person who appears at various important events; [from a character in the 1983 film *Zelig*]

zeptosecond one sextillionth of a second

Zerzura Oasis a rumored city that may have existed in some form deep in the Sahara desert in western Egypt or Libya; AKA The Oasis of Little Birds, the city was said to have a sleeping king & queen and be white as a dove, full of treasure, and guarded by giants

Zeta Draconis a binary star in the northern circumpolar constellation Draco – old name Aldhibah; [Arabic *Al Dhi'bah* (the she-wolf)]

zoetic pertaining to life; alive

Zone of Avoidance or **Zone of Galactic Obscuration** an area of the sky that is obscured by the center of our galaxy (the Milky Way) and thus difficult for astronomers to observe objects beyond it

zonked very tired; deep asleep; drunk; [slang]

zoomorphic having an animal's shape or likeness; relating to or being a deity in animal form

Zyrian a Finnic language

Zyzzyva the genus of a tropical American snouted beetle; [so named to be the last word in most dictionaries]

Supplemental Words of Beauty or Interest

To keep this book concise, definitions for these words are *not* provided. The meaning of many entries are relatively apparent, but some are quite obscure. (*Quantum chromodynamics* falls squarely within the latter category.) A writer (or anyone who wanted to engrain these beautiful words into their memory) could scan this section a few times, perhaps highlighting favorites. Please consider this a separate, concise, nine-page resource within this volume that hopefully many will find useful and/or inspiring. (Multi-word entries are *italicized*.)

abysm abyssal acclivity acropolis adieux Adonic adultescent aegis aeonian aerie affinitive afflation affluential aflower aflutter aftercast afterclap after-days afterdeck afterglow afterlight afterwit afterworld afteryears agasp ageless aghast agleam aglimmer aglisten ahungered air-castle airfaring alacrity albescent alchemical alchemystical alfresco alienist alpenglow alpenhorn alpenstock alpestrine altocumuli *amaranth purple* ambrosiac ambrosial *amethystine python* ammoniac amnestic amorphous *anabelian geometry* anharmonic *annus mirabilis* answerless anthemic *antique green* aplomb apotheosis apparition aqueous aquiline aquiver arboreous arborescent arboresque arcane archangelic ardencies Argus-eyed aria ascendant ashimmer ashiver aspirant *astral plane* *astronomical twilight* astrophile astrosphere asunder aswarm athrill athrong athwart Audenesque august aureate aurorean auriferous avatar aviatress aviatrix avifauna awash awheel awhirl axemaster azureous azurine bacchanalian balletic *ballistic magnetoresistance* banner-cloud bantling barbaresque baronial barrowman bastardry *Beast of Exmoor* *beam wind* beautied becarpeted bechance becharm becloud becrown bedarken bedewed bedwork befoam begirdle begloom beleaguered *belle epoque* bellygod belvedere

bemadden bemazed bemonstered bemusements
benighted bereft beshadow bespoke bestial *bete noire*
betoken betwixt bicorporal birdlore birdmen birdsong
bitangent bitchcraft blackguard blackwash blandishments
blinkered bloodstroke blusterous bogart bonhomie
bookcraft booklore bootless boscage branchway
brave west winds bromidic brownshort *Brunswick blue*
bucolic bulbacious bullyrook bumbledom *burnt ocher*
bushcraft Byronically Byronics Byzantine cacophonous
cadaverous Camelot campcraft cannibalic caper-cutting
caperous *Capri blue* capric capricious carcass-roofing
Carpathian lynx Caspian snowcock Castilian brown
catacomb caterwaul catharsis caverned cavernicolous
celerity celestial celestine centaur centuried cerulean
chasmic Cherubim chivalresque choleric chopfallen
chunder circumambient circumambulate circumaviate
circumboreal circumclusion circumferentially circumfluent
circumgyratory circumpolar circumstanced *circumstellar
disc* circumvallate *cirrostratus nebulosus* cleave clerisy
clandestine cloudage cloud-born cloud-built cloudburst
cloudcapt cloud-drift *cloud forest* cloud-kissing cloudlands
cloudscape cloudwashed cloud-woven coarsening
coastland cockloft cocksman codestream coextensive
cognoscenti comport concatenation conflated confluence
*confluent hypergeometric function Conspiracy of the Fire
Cells* contradistinction conundrum coruscating
cosmocentric cosmopolis coterie courtcraft countercharm
countercoup counterglow counterphobic countershot
counterspy countervail craftless cragsman craven
creedsman crepusculous *crescent dune crescent terrapin*
crestfallen crevasse *Crimian Goths crimson sunbird*
croftland crowdsensing cryogenic cryosphere crystalline
cumuli cupidity curl-cloud cutlass cyberian cygnet
Cygnus Star Cloud Czechlands dalesman Daliesque
damask Daneland darkling darkening darksome
dastardized daughterboard dauntless daymare daysail

daysleeper deathling decadescent decorous deepening deliriant dell deluge demesne demigoddess demilune demitint deportment desacrilized descry desultorious detritus *deus ex machina* dewbeam dewbow dewdropped dewfall dewy-eyed *Diana monkey* diaphanous diluvial diluvium dimmity *Diophantine geometry* discommodious disconsolate discountenance disembowered disenthrall disgorged disporting dispraised disprivacied disquiet dogmata dolorous dotardly draconian dracontine draggletailed dram dreambound dreameries dreamful dreamingly dreamlands dreamlessly dreamscape dream-stricken dreamwork dreamwrapt dreamy-souled dulcet dulcifying dunelands dustfall dustmote echelon echoic echoless edgestone efferent eiderdown *élan vital* eld eldritch elfinwood elfland elflock *elf owl* elixir elsehow elsewhen elusory elven embayed emblossom embowered embracive embreathe embronze emmarble empierce emplume empress encaged enchained encharm encipher encloud endarkening endpleasure enfolden enforest enfrenzied engarlanded engender engild engirdling englacial engrailed engreening enkindling enlacement enrapt enravish enripening enshaded enshroud enskied enslaven enthrone entomb envenom envisage *ephemeris time epic simile* epiphanic epochal equanimous equidimensional equiform equinoctial erg erstwhile *esoteric cosmology* especial esplanade eternize ether *ethereal blue* etherish ethos euphonious euphonic euphoriant evanescent evenfall evenlight evensong evetide everliving exclosure excrescence exemplar exfiltrate extragalactic extrospection eyebeam fabulist fadelessly fairyland fairylore *false map turtle* fancywork fantasque fathomless featherhead featherly feckless felinity fernland *Findhorn Ecovillage* finespun finiteless firebolt *fire cloud* fireflied firestorm flaxen fledgling fleeced fleeciness fleshling floriferous floriform florisitic flowerage flowstone flummox flyaway flybridge flyspecked foliaged footfall forebrain forechosen foredeck foredoom foredunes forefeeling foreglimpse foreknown forelands forelock foremothers forename forenoon forepleasure forespoken foreworld *forest bathing* forestland forestless foretaste foretime foretoken forlorn formicate fraught freshet frond frostbound frostbow frostwork frothy fungacious futurity gabbling *galactic bulge* gambol garth genderfluid *genius loci* geostrategic ghastly ghostland ghostless ghostshipping gibberbird gibbering gigglemug *glacier snout* glaciofluvial glade glamourpuss gleamings gleamless glimmerings glitterance gloam gobsmacked goditorium gold-bright *golden-feather yellow* *golden hour* goose-stepper gossamer graceless grandiloquent graupel graven greeneries green-fingered greenscape greensward greenway greenwood grief-shot grotesquerie groupthink growlery gutterblood gyre gyrotrigonometry halcyonian *Harmonic Convergence* *harmonic interval* *harpy eagle* havenless haversack havocking hegira helioseismic hellbred hellbroth hemispheric herblore *hermosa pink* *heroic verse* *hibernian green* highflown highveld hillstream hillwalker hindbrain hindermost hinterland hobohemia *holomorphic function* honeyed honey-tongued horizonless hornwork *hyperbolic geometry* *Iberian lynx* iceblink icebound icefall icescape icelight *ideal realism* idyllic ignifluous ilk ill-disposed illimitable illiterati ill-scented ill-starred illume illuminant illuminative Illuminati illusory imbastardized imbreathe imbrue imbrute imbue imitatrix immantle immesh immingle immix impalement impalpable impark impasse impenitent *imperial purple* imperil imperious impish impling implumed imponderable impuissant inburnt inburst incantation incarnadine incarnate incontestable indecorous indelicate indrift ineffable ingress inimical inimitable inkslinger innumerable inordinately inquietude inquisitorial insensate insouciant insuperable intangible interfingering interfluent interfulgent interlace

interlardment interleave interlude intermesh
interpenetrate interstage interstice intertangling invariant
inviolable iridescent iron-fisted ironhearted isinglass
isoperimetric ivied jasper jazzy *joie de vivre* joust
junoesque juvenescent juxtaposing Kafkaesque kingcraft
kismet knell knight-errant *La-La Land* labyrinthine
lacewood lacework lachrymose lactiferous lakehead
lakeland lakelore lamasery lambent landloper landreeve
landsman languorous *lapis lazuli* lardaceous lassitude
lasslorn lattermath latticework *laughing owl* lavafall
lavender gray lavish lawyerball lea leaflitter legionary
legislatrix lenshound leonine liegeless lifesome lifestream
lifeway lightsome lilac liliaceous lilyturf limpid lionize
liquescent lissome literati littermate liturgic loci longspun
looky-loo loreless lotusland louche lovelock lovelorn
lovemap lucent luciferous lucre luculent ludomania
lugubrious *lumiere green* luminary luminescence
luminiferous luminous lunabase lunisolar lupine lurid
luscious *MacGregor's giant honeyeater* *madder crimson*
madding madrigal maelstrom magmata magmatic
magnetohydrodynamics mammiferous *mansard roof*
mantlerock *map lichen* marginalia matchless matriculate
mazed mazily mazy mead meadowland meadowlark
meadowless meatspace medulla megaparsec
Meistersinger melancholic melange mellific memelord
memorabilities memoried memosphere mercurial
mesmeric meta metagalactic metamathematical
metathesis miasmic midheaven mien milieux millennian
mindflow mindscape mindstream miraged mireland
mirrored mirrorless mirrorshades miserabilist mishmosh
mistbow *mizzen skysail* moanworthy moilsome moldering
money-ridden *monkey puzzle tree* *monkey tail cactus*
monstricide montage moodscape moonbeam moondust
moongaze moonglow moonling moonsail moonscape
moonsickle moonstricken moonwashed mooseyard
morbid moribund morningtide morrowtide mosaicked

mossy maze polypore mothercraft *mountain lilac* muci multisonous munificent murksome murmurless museless myselves mysterial mysteried mysticity mystification mystique mythos nacreousness nameless nares nascent nauseant nebulochaotic nebulous necromantic necropolis necropolitan nectareal nectarous neophiliac nethers nethermind netherworld *neva green* nexus nightblooming night-cloud nightfall night-faring nightglow nightscape nightwandering nimbiferous nimbus nirvanic nivometric nonchalance nonpareil nonplussed nookeries nook-shotten *Norwegian Forest cat* numberless numerable nympholeptic oblivial oblivions obsidian ocular odditorium oddsboard odoriferous odorprint ombibulous omnicompetent omnificent omnilucent omnipatient omnipresent omnistrain omniverse *opalescent sea slug opera pink* optionality oracular orchidaceous otherworldly otiose oubliette outdream outgleam outlander outredden outré outsweeten outworld overbold overbrooding overclass overdaring overdog overgild overgloom overkingdom overmoist overpeopled overperch overponderous overquell overraking overshine oversoul overstink oversummer overture overveil overworld owleries owl-eyed owlish oxblood *pale indigo* palliative pallid pancosmic pandemonious pangless panharmonic Panslavonian pantherine pantingly pantoscopic pantropical paradigmatic paradimensional paradisal paradisiac paragon parallactic parallelless *parametric equations* paramour paranormality parapet parquetry passthought pasturage pathos peacocking peerless Pegasean pellmell pendulous penumbra perchance percipient percussive perdurable performative perilune perimetric periwinkles persiflage phallocentric pharaonic phasma philanthrobber phlegmatic phosphoreous piggery pineclad *pink fairy armadillo* piratical piscifauna plashy plateaux *pleasing fungus beetle* plenilune plethora plexus plumeless pluvial pneumatic poesy poltergism

ponderosities portend portentous postbellum postdiluvian
pratfall praxis precipitous preterlapsed primacy primeval
prismatic prosaic prosy protean protofascist protogalactic
protohuman protomartyr protomorphic protoplasmic
protosun provenance *Prussian blue* psychophysics
pudenda puerile pulchrify pupatation *purple fringeless
orchid* purse-proud purulent pygmean Pythonesque
quafftide quaggy quagmire qualmless *quantum
chromodynamics* quasicrystalline quasiperiodicity quaver
queencraft queenliness quell quenchless quicksilver
quill pig quintessential quisling quixotic raffish railbird
rainbowed rainshadow rakish rarify ravage ravenous
raving razorable *recreational mathematics red junglefowl
Redbone Coonhound* redolent reflower refractive refulgent
rejuvenescent relumine remembrancer remunerable
renascent requiem residuum rhapsodic rhinocerial
rhombitrihexagonal tiling rime ripsnorter riven rodentia
romancy romanticist roofscape ruinosity ruinous runecraft
runesmith runic sacrosanct saffron sagacious sailplane
saintstress salacious salamandrine salient sandscape
sandspout sapience saporific sapphired saturnine satyr
saunterings scansioned scanties scintillant scriptorium
seaborn seaborne seabound seacoast seacraft seagirt
seamount seaquake sea-roving seascape sea-wolf
sea-worn seemings semblative semipellucid semisomnia
semisphere senescent senex sennight sensorial
sequacious serendipity serpentine shadowlands
shadowless shadowy sheathe Shelleyan *Shelley's eagle owl*
shimmering shorelark shroudless sibilant siegecraft
siegeworks silhouetted singular skifield skirling
skull-collecting ant sky green skyborne skybound
Skydaddy skyey skyfaring skyflower skyglow skylacing
skylarking skyless skylighted skyline skysail skyscapes
skywalk skywritten slabstone slacktivist *slake trough*
slakeless slanguage slaughterhall sleekstone sleepbound
slipstream slumberless slumberous smokeshow *snail cloud*

sneezeweed snoutfair snowblink snowclad snowcraft
snowface snowscape snowtopped somniferous somnolent
songcraft songless sonneteer sonoluminescence sonorous
soporific spadework spannew spate spatterwork specter
spectra *spectral bat* spectrality speechcraft spellbound
spellcraft spellfire spermatophobia spheral sphinctered
sphincteric spirituous springtide spume spumiferous
stagecraft starlight starsailing starscape starshine
starvelings statecraft *Steller's sea ape Steller's sea eagle*
stellify stone-cast stonecraft stonefall stone-hearted
stoneless stoneweed stonework stormbound stormcock
storm-lashed stormwind strandhound stratocirrus
stupefacient suavities *sub rosa* subadolescent sublimities
submatrix submontane subsumed subtransparent
suckhole sudatorium suffuse summered summerless
summertide sumptuary sunbeam sunbow sunbreak
sunburst suncapped sundart sunder sunderable sunfall
sunfilled sunglade sunglint sunglow sunkissing sunrist
sunshaft sun-shot sunshower sunstone sunswept
superbeing supercelestial supine surprisal suspire
suspiration swanship sward swordcraft sybaritic tactile
tarn tenebrous tentacular *the aftertimes* thermogravimetric
thoughtform thoughtworld thralldom threnody
thunderblast thunderbolt thunderless thunderpeal
thundersnow thundersquall thunderstone thunderstroke
thundrous tincture *titanium white* titian titillative
topgallant staysail topazine tornadic torpid torrid
transcendental number theory transfluent translucent
translucid travertine travesty treescape tremulant
tremulous trident triflorous trilemma triste tristful
trouserless truepenny tumulus tuneless tussockland
twilighted twilitten twinborn *Tyrian purple* ubiquity
ultracold *ultraparallel theorem* umber umbragacious
umbral calculus unblooded unbosom uncompanioned
undawning undercolor undergrove underlick undernote
undersea undersky underthings underween undulate

unfellowed unfledged unfrequented ungirt unhorsed unmuzzle unparagoned unplumbed unquelled unquiet unrevenued unseemly unshadowed unshriven unstudied unsummered untoward untrammeled untraveled unutterable upslanting utopian vacuity vagary vale vampiric vastity veldfire vellum *Venetian glass* venturesome verboten verdant verdurous vernal *Veronese green* versecraft versification vertex vertiginous vestigial viatic vicissitudinous victrix vineland vineries vinquish violaceous violescent viperous vipress vitriform visage viscount vividity vivification vixenish voiceless volant volitant voluminous vulgarian waft warlight wavefolding weft weirdward whalesong whence whiffler whirlygigs windfallen windjammer windlashed windstrewn windthrow windwheel wine-dark wineland winelore wintertide wistful witling wonder-bearing wonderbeast wonderberry wonderglow wonderkind wonderland wondershine wonderworld wondrous woodfern woodland woodlore wowless wraithlike wreathe wunderkind yoctosecond yestern yesternight yeti yonderly youthquake zephyrus zephyrean *zinc green*

THE END

About the Author
Robin Devoe is the *nom de plume* of Rob E. Earl – an Alaskan who enjoys word-collecting, poetry, skiing, cycling, and motorcycling. Past volumes include *Dictionary of the Strange, Curious, and Lovely* (2017) and *Pale Western Star: The Poetry of Robin Devoe* (2019).

Printed in Great Britain
by Amazon

f1eb3a26-0712-439e-a0b2-65d47b39ae73R02